IMAGINE HERE

IMAGINE HERE

Edited by Kelly Olsen

First published in Great Britain in 1998 by Poetry
Today, an imprint of
Penhaligon Page Ltd, 12 Godric Square, Maxwell Road,
Peterborough. PE2 7JJ

A Catalogue record for this book is available from the
British Library.

ISBN 186226 026

Typesetting and layout, Penhaligon Page Ltd, England.
Printed and bound by Forward Press Ltd, England

Foreword

Imagine Here is a compilation of poetry, featuring some of our finest poets. The book gives an insight into the essence of modern living and deals with the reality of life today. We think we have created an anthology with a universal appeal.

There are many technical aspects to the writing of poetry and *Imagine Here* contains free verse and examples of more structured work from a wealth of talented poets. To choose winners from the wide range of styles and forms is a most difficult task, albeit a pleasurable one. On this occasion, the winners are as follows:

S Stouppa	Dedicated to the Aged Lady of Moorme
R Bevan	Bully Hill
S Wagener	Microcosm
B Tyree	Grandfather's Roses
W Greig	Swimming Pool Date

My congratulations and thanks go to them and to all of you who have contributed to *Imagine Here,* and I trust you will enjoy it as much as I have.

Contents

The Poems

Ignorantia Legis
Paul G Gowland

If Godstruck be periodic
Eden warlock renuke his frame.
Pie in sky imperial imprints
One cloud? Yes! Two . . Three . . . Nine . . .

More anon, a must in origin
Consigning clowns unto their bunks.
A tom cat astra free falls earthward
Godstruck halls of glory found.

Sin ominous rolling wheat-like
August wind spawned butcherous creed.
Sun, rain, snow and shadow sibling
Particulate incandescent dust.

Terror firmer and fervour tremouring
Cast inside your crustacean shell.
An organic exo-gild of bark
Still old bells ring so young.

Krish nappeased by domino blocks
Of sapien sapien tonnes de force.
Alpha and Omega if Godstruck now
How periodic would all our wars?

Colours (Of Adamawa State)
Julia Rumbold

Harmattan dust covers the hills
draining them of colour and definition
like a poor quality grainy photograph.
Once green grass shines golden pink
some stacked in bundles
leaning against newly thatched houses.
A cracked pot lies abandoned
waiting
to return to the terra-cotta earth.
Burnt rocks and singed saplings
blackened by bush fire
darken the road side.

Best clothes, bright cloth,
gifts on heads, babies on backs,
friends walk along side each other,
chatting,
in the direction of the gathering.

White cotton bols freshly picked
spilling out of stuffed stacks,
waiting
to be sealed and sewn.
The crimson coke truck with wobbling crates
struggles nervously up the hill.
On to Yola.

London: Opus '69
Alex Marsh

pigeon perches, taking seed
from a small white cup, sixpence a feed.

nelson's perching, watching london
trafalgar's over, cos You're not there.

You laughed at all the pigeons as they stalked around Your feet;
danced in the rainbow of the fountains spray;
challenged all the lions to a battle in westminster;
later, at westminster, You cried, because they'd gone.

dirty thames in a full tripping steamer,
running down the sightsandsounds;
You kissed me then, as never before, in so soft and full a kiss,
that nelson closed his other eye.

under housesroadsandgardens,
moaning through the caves of steel;
dimlit stations, light oases,
faceless people.

same old rain at our destination,
over the common to that small coffee bar.

if I could preserve one moment of You,
it would be then as You smiled in a coffeeflavoured smile;
and Your eyes,
even now they make my heart leap, for the memory lifts my soul.

now I walk the londonstreets,
I hear You call me but it's a hotdogseller;
I see Your face on the other train that's going the other way;
all the galleries paintings have Your words tattooed around them.

a sad cafe, still with Your laughter echoing softly
and the pigeons won't eat from my hand any more.
Trafalgar's over.

Bothen Hill
Sharon Muhl

Give me the scent of the Bluebell Wood.
The sound of wind singing through trees.
Show me leaves dappled with bright sun light.
A golden copse studded with butterfly wing.

Let me have the seasons flow.
A dewy field
A blanket of white on white snow.
All I need is Nature's gift
Of summer flowers and now at last
The sweet sweet breath of spring.

Dedicated To The Aged Lady of Moormeads
S M Stouppa

In leisured stroll,
On one sun-sprung day,
Across the confined
Pleasures of a local green,
I saw with one dimension's eyes
The families that passed me by
All captured as in some harmony
Of peace and seeming tranquillity
And all around this oasis
Lay, layer upon layer of antithesis.
But much preferring
A cameo view
Noticed the skylight's vaulted blue
And with what delicacy
The bare-laced trees
Etched patterns with the passing breeze
And how the sun
Intensified the scene
To one of darkest emerald green
And how the willow, weeping
In its tattered yellowed-green gown,
Draws the ever hungry eye
To the river slipping by
And how the conifers and
Evergreens
Stand everlastingly serene
As railway's trains go clicking by
And aeroplanes, that have learnt to fly,
Criss cross over in the sky
Like angry buzzing flies
Not to mention various breeds,
Of four legged varieties.

Special Place
Caroline Isherwood

In the lofty cathedral of the trees
Where shafts of lambent golden light
Pour down in singing arcs of brilliance
Through living pillars of abraded bark;
Where nodding blooms of pristine white
And blue, and upturned sunburst petals,
Burst to view, nestling amid soft mattresses
Of vibrant emerald moss and tender shoots of fern;
Here, in tangled mounds of briars
Where burgeoning pale spires of green
Swiftly climb the scaffolding of the old years growth
To form vast sanctuaries for the building
Of new homes from the wreckage of the old;
Here, where the rush of weed-clouded streams
Play Pan-pipe music from their rocky beds
To swell the choir of birds,
Whose fledglings scatter the waters
of their baptism to the thirsty forest floor;
Here is a special place.

The Perfect Place For Lovers
S Hussey

They dipped their feet in the sparkling stream
Catching their breath as the chill caught them unaware
Clutching each other, stumbling onto grassy tufts by the brook,
Laughing, in this perfect place for lovers.

The colours of autumn, burnished and golden,
Glowed against bracken and purple-capped hills.
Their gazes lingered and locked, and they slumbered in each others

arms

Dreaming, in this perfect place for lovers.

But years have moved onwards and the passage of time
Has brought a longing for those years they'd once known.
These companions with memories now dimming, receding,
Wondering, about that perfect place for lovers.

Now their journey is over, the decades roll back,
Their faded eyes survey a scene of ravages
Wrought in a concrete world. A car park, a kiosk, the fumes and the

noise,

No longer a perfect place for lovers.

At The Bottom Of Brixton Hill
Sophie Breese

Just friends
Just sitting
In Brixton
We're chatting
And considering
Different standpoints
From our table
On the pavement
And we're drinking
Cool beer
Since it's summer
And we're here
And so time
Slowly passes
While we drink
A few more glasses
And the music
Gets louder
As the people
Start to gather
Round the entrance
To the night-club
We're next door to
At the hub of
We're both hoping
But not protesting
Skirting round
The awkward issue
That perhaps
The gentle flirting
Will develop
Into a kiss
This is Brixton
In the summer
And soon we will be
More than just friends

Bassenthwaithe: A Sonnet
Terence Stacey

Rugged hills gleam under the auspices of
autumnal sun; brocken spectres crawl and creep
over ridges near Bassenthwaite, the long lake seeps
into gravel at our feet, we cast aloft
stones, arcing into Dame du Lacs deep domain.
Your cobalt eyes have a gaze of ice in them,
my lorelei love; the lake is still, again -
lip claps echo, I clutch your strawberry mane.
Lake-bound archipelagos act as gull - homes
their siren calls make you smile at my unease-
birds aren't my forte: ancestors of diseased
creatures long deceased. The gulls laugh and screech like crones.
We do not mention my limp petrifaction,
you laugh tears of callousness and jubilation.

A Midsummer Night In Tettenhall
Andrew J Detheridge

The suicidal sun plunged out of the sky
As a company of actors
Changed from teachers and solicitors
To lovers and fairies.

As the moon stalked through the lower branches,
Wolverhampton was briefly transformed
Into a balmy Athenian evening
As Theseus tenderly wooed his Amazonian bride.

For a few, swift-footed hours,
From the red-rose mechanicals
To the glittered and leotarded fairies
And the caped lovers
(with their dew-rusted swords)
Time was but a comet across the heavens.

Then, as the tinsel stars laughed
At the silliest stuff below
And the iron tongue of midnight
Licked at their heels
All too soon
Did the lovers to bed,
Did the breathless Puck forgiveness beg,
Did Moonshine draw breath to snuff out his candle
Did the laughter fall and nestle on the whispering leaves,
Did Athens fade back into the blackened night.

The Old Mill
B J Bull

Through the wooded glen, at
    Talybont
The Ysgethin flows.
Its bouldered way down to the
    sea
A fairy tale unfolds.
Trees of splendid hue bow down,
Netted sunbeams dance
And many a stream goes
    wandering off
Its fortunes there to chance.

There's one such stream that
    gurgles down
Under the road and round,
Through a meadow green to an
    Old Mill's wheel
Whose beats no longer sound.
The Old Mill's wheel stands still
    as stone,
Its work in life is done,
No more the Millers daughter
    grinds,
No more the Carter's come.

Its cobwebbed beams of oaken
    strength
And greying stones of old,
Beside a tranquil stream now
    stand,
That once a torrent flowed.
Then darkness falls and bats
    trapeze
Nocturnal swoops of joy.
Their flurried flight is often seen

Beneath a moonlit sky.

And upwards on to Bodlyn Lake,
You may perchance to see,
A lovers knot grows strongly yet
In some secluded tree.
In summertime the warm winds
        blow,
the grass grows tall and green,
A hundred years go tumbling by,
Still nature reigns supreme.

Sunbeams slant from mountain
        top
Then gently softly pause,
On banks of moss and stretching
        fern
Which girth the rivers course.
And down below the furrowed
        sea
Sighs with tenderness.
Upon this life that's now sublime,
And not a wilderness.

Nowhere In Particular
Carla Pinhey

Distant and surreal. Absent and unknown.
Familiar yet vaguely unrecognisable
the land my life is a pilgrimage to.
There is no map, no way of knowing
which direction or path to follow.

Fields of green and rivers of blue
role through the fictional landscape.
Vivid creations of perfection
float aimlessly through the tangled
jungle of my disillusioned mind.

the nucleus of my paragon
essentially is nothing more than
the essence of a poetical vision.
Realism is forgotten and buried
beneath all that is supremely legendary.

The Boulevard
Frank Samet

Staring beechwood on dusty forms
The leaves, the rich coffee fumes
Wafting in happy solace
Gracing the noses

The swallows are all flying
In explicable circles
And the moon too early for the sunset
Looms pale

Expensive perfumes and crowned ivory smiles
Linger far on into the night
Setting the scene
For all to follow

The bare shouldered women
Suck long peaceful cigarettes
Whilst the men sip liquors
And out-stare the universe

The lap dogs skip for cake
And are loved by the woman
Whose fleshy jewelled fingers
Know precisely how to caress

The one-armed pavement artist
Chalks his final mark
For people to drop their money
Into his black beret and kids

The night is now thin
And the only warmth
Comes from drinking
Raw cognac

And all this I saw with a tired heart
But could not form and response
That had died within me a long time ago
So sad

From a wooden bench I saw
A waiter picking up broken glass
And a manager gently helping
A man steady himself for home

Where Cornfields Grow
Gemma Stunden

Opaque, I walk through the grey days passing.
My foot falls soft upon their hostile shores.
But I will take you to where cornfields grow:
Countless golden heads, fleshy with summer
And the promises of harvest plenty,
Laced with the shy jewels of nature's garden.
Born on the weathered palm of this dry land,
Fragile rubies flutter butterfly wings.
Sapphire buds, demurely contoured, gaze up
At the glint of shining amethyst stars.

And I will build a house of red sand brick,
A haven to shadow the swollen sun,
Where we may sit and review our book of days
And watch poppy seed birds scatter across
A cornflower sky. Blue light trailing, flow
Down the fissures of dusk, to indigo.
Though stood in the half light of days passing,
Each sense fills with the fragrance of cornfields,
And as we walk through our nature's garden
My foot sinks deep into the native earth.

Disappearing Act
Nicola Wood

Refuge in illusion.
shelter from reality.
These four walls
are all.

Escapism is real–
an ideal ideology.

No vanishing tricks.
No magic mirrors.
Just four walls,
and me.

Me and my disappearing act.

Windmill Hill Guide Camp
Jennie Dawes

Little Guides with kit-bags, leaped from fathers' cars
Anxious to pitch camp and sleep beneath the stars
Tin mugs, bedrolls, billy-cans, voices loud and shrill
We clattered up the trodden path to HQ Windmill Hill!

Intense evening sunshine burned thro' our royal blue
Roll call, drill, inspection, each allotted tasks to do
Some crawled under canvas and inserted big tent poles
We fetched wood and lit the fire in Mistletoe patrol!

Some were wielding mallets to hammer wooden pegs
And soon had whacking bruises on knuckles thumbs & legs!
Fran sneaked to the village and bought supplies of tuck
The Foxgloves got 'ablutions' - what really rotten luck!

Whistle signals, tying knots, stalking through the wood
Identifying trees and birds, I practised when I could
I felt reliable and strong in pumps and last year's shorts
To be dependable and wise were my only thoughts

So serious and sensible for 'Taps' we gathered round,
Stood a moment quietly, our eyes fixed on the ground
Plaits and freckles, teenage limbs turning golden brown
In the last rays of the sunset our Standard lowered down

'Now for a game of rounders' our young Lieutenant said
'Soup for supper round the fire, a singsong, and to bed'
Then giggling and undressing, flashing torches in the dark
And letting Captain's guy ropes down, was really quite a lark!

Our hilarity was in full swing round about midnight,
When suddenly her furious face gave us such a fright
Illuminated by the moon, in cold cream and hairpins
Framed within our tentflap we jumped out of our skins!

I remember every moment of our camp among the trees,
The dappled greens, the horseflies, a lisping summer breeze
Sausages and wood smoke, stout staffs and bits of string
For making wobbly gadgets no good for anything!

Our wet feet in the morning dew, blackberries and beans,
Earwigs in our sleeping bags and what 'Team Spirit' means
How with our little penknives we sharpened sticks to points
Polished badges, belts and shoes and bandaged up our joints!

And in the evening twilight, when we'd done all the chores,
Our piping voices rendering 'The Quartermasters Stores'
Sunburnt grimy faces, glowing round the big camp fire
We were the happiest Girl Guides in all of Nottinghamshire!

Bridge of Love
Julie Irene Baker

Out there in the world
wherever you may be,
at any time, you can think
of me.
Just a thought away
just a blink of the eye
no need for tears no need
to cry.
Your soul is mine
mine is yours
in our minds there are
no doors.
Just a bridge of love
from me to you
you can cross it
and I can too.
So close your eyes
and you will see
a vision of someone
that someone is me.

Visit To Saint Julian's
Jan Porter

Waterlily days,
Spangled light-on-water days.

Poised, there seemed only this -
an interplay of light and shadow
lasting ten whole days.

As in a dream I came here,
crossed over the smooth, clear lawn,
passed round smiles fine and delicate
as Sunday sandwiches,
uttered words almost forgotten
into the airy, undecked chapel.
Then fell into bed like a child,
waking to the tiny summer sounds -
martins and swallows
diving past lattice windows;
the sun sifting across my breakfast tray,
spilling my cup-and-saucer with marigold.

Bolton Priory
Catherine Orchard

I saw Bolton Priory in the rain,
Through a gap in an old stone wall
As if, part of the past, in a picture frame.
Tall and simple and open to the sky
With slim arched windows of stone
That let the sky through
And looked out in silence to survey
A world of beauty and greyness too
Of moorland merging with the fading light
Reached through meadows of dying green
With bare outlines of the leafless trees,
Grey and full the rising stream,
The Priory grey and empty as a shell
Yet an austere beauty in the silent scene.
As I gazed I wondered what might have been
In the abundance of the summer months
With monks in rough homespun gowns,
And scientists, physicians, writers and artists
Untouched by the confused ignorant world
Far from the haunts of men, in a world forever green,
Freely obeying their inner spiritual needs
With a simplicity of life and a love of solitude
Part of the earth like the pillars and trees
Fulfilled as the windows of heavenly light
Beneath arches delicate as summer leaves.
Their gifts from above they created again
Gave their lives back to God in their art
A witness I stand of an age of creation
An age of the past that still stirs the heart.

Wicklow Night
Damien McAuley

When night comes to this house
All huddle up on favoured chairs.
It is truly black outside.
Tilley is hanging from the ceiling.

Words out and romance is at its peak
fog clings to the windows outside.
Willows sigh and quietly converse
The path is stone, cold.
Ants wriggle up and under
Their bodies tighten with excitement.
The light creates an area outside.
These ants love the seasons and the people that come with them.

It's so far an owl would hoot.
I hear something, a growing something.
Witnessing the formation of this land
Oh there are hairs standing all around
Post Meridiem in Ireland.

As morning comes, it appears
Then it looks just like a little white pebble
An egg placed on to a green table cloth and with its weight, sinks.

Nature
Jeff Chick

A flower born of nature,
Covered by the first frost.
If it were to be picked or
By one gentle touch,
All would be lost.

September Song
Irving Parry

Lace curtains of spume sway across the loch.
Trees bend in obeisance to the wind.
Falling leaves in panic run amok.
Soft, siren screams invade the conscious mind.

Deep sadness at summer's passing fills the heart.
Her lush abundance safely garnered in
She leaves, reluctant to depart.
And I am lonely. Empty from within.

Gathering birds compact the singing lines
Then rise as one in fast formating flocks.
Flee south to warming, kinder climes.
'Tis winter's Herald: the autumn Equinox.

For What We Have Received
A'O'E

The blossom hearted trees burst
Into a bombardment of colour leaf and petals,
That drift on the bracing April wind.
I want to flick a switch,
To stop the time and place and hold it just for me.
Not having it to share it, or trite comment make.
I say it every year in case it is my last.
No place or setting, nor jewel or man made thing.
Can be as beautiful as England in the spring.

The Place
Yvonne Finch

Had this once been the place?
The solitary place to which we came.
Its hush unbroken but for sensuous cuckoo's call
in early spring,
and rasp of cricket heard in dry and dusty summer grass
that burned to hay.

This once had been the place.
The solitary place to which men came
with implements of noise to desecrate, rip-open earth, destroy,
and bury all
beneath foundation tomb-stones, geometric order rising
row on row.

When we had known the place,
that solitary place to which we came,
we never knew it would implant some essence of itself in us
so deep.
A gentle backcloth to our childhood, special, poignant,
sweet.

Now close in silent shared regret, we turned away but wondered
why it was
we felt this sudden flash of feeling only when we knew its
loss.

She Is The Sea
Emma Wiseman

Sinuous,
Like a snake,
Coiling and uncoiling;
Like a cat,
Rushing to greet you,
And then rushing away again.
Dancing with carefree joy
To a rhythm only she can hear.
Bejewelled by the sun,
Caressed by the winds,
The heavens rush down to greet her.
Surrounded by silent sentinels,
The cliffs are her guardians;
She curls herself at their feet.
Yet her calls are unheard.
Angry now, she throws herself
Against the walls of her prison
As if to beat them down -
A child throwing a tantrum.
Spent, exhausted,
Her rage subsides,
And the waves are still once more.

Fingers In The Mist
Joan Broad

Whispering fingers through the mist
Touching, caressing,
Softly stroking,
Awakes the feelings long repressed

Whispering fingers through the mist.
Finds the places,
And heart races
In anticipated touch of lips

Whispering fingers through the mist
Touch more strongly,
Feelings responding,
Passion rising to the tips.

Whispering fingers through the mist,
Gently holding
Loving feelings,
Flow through bodies in the mist.

Soulless In Rhondda
Ellis

A stubborn wind blows gently over the resplendent, mercurial valley
Gadding through those madding, undulating hills with gay abandon
To roll translucently across unspanned crags nearby bubbling stream
Where bream and trout meander melancholy, amid charismatic,
reed
tipped pathways, of icy cold, pebble stoned, sunspeckled white water

Out, from a scarlet ravine, gashed 'midst a purple heather tinted hue
The mighty predator soars majestically, below puff pillowed clouds
on
ecclasiasical wings propelled by God pursed lips, in search of his
prey
While a snow dappled silken soft field mouse, innocently winds
along
her way, to a subterranean safehouse in a damson peach glowed
grotto

Hark, to the dark stalwart souls still waiting on solitary cemetery
mount
Whose love was not as strong willed as their strait laced predecessors
And therefore did not find enigmatic happiness or peace above
mortality
Nor the rain spattered, grey slate covered, long streeted, ill lit,
erstwhile,
somesay servile, but extremely volatile, stereo typed community
below

NOW in the chapel barn houses, abides modern software singular
family
Where once mounted sermons rang through multitudinous
congregation
Ever obedient with an understanding, tragically forever sadly
longlost
To a cataclysmic degeneration and rejection, inbred of another time
now

bygone past, never to be choired heavenwards on larkspun voices
again

Young, I was then, hobnailed and coalfilled, uncaring as I leapt
joyously
Around bracken crackled, green carpeted, wool adorned luchy
pastures
Never thinking, that one day, all this presrdained intoxication must
end
And that the dark sky veil, slinkily slipsliding wearily down this
drabbed
worn out husk, would soon obliterate a lifetime of fondly recalled
memory
INSTANTLY

A stubborn wind again blows gently over the resplendent, mercurial
valley
Along with my fellow travellers I stand chained in the longest
tarblack line
Awaiting patiently for deaths sombre appearance on dank, cemetery
mount
Did I love, or believe enough, to warrant this impending sojourn to
infinity
Or, like the sad God forsaken wretches watching despondently in
poignant
shadows, will I forever seek out absolution for my rebellious,
haunted soul

Vienna 1830
W Bagwell

Waltzes in the deep of night
While wind blows round the frosty eves
Are written crouched by candle light
And pages fall like autumn leaves

The music that is in my head
I cannot quite get in the score
In anguish bite my lips that bled
And dripped from paper onto floor

My spirits grey just like the dawn
My drooping sagging limbs too spent
Now yet to face another morn
No bartered tune to pay the rent

I Am

Ben Weston

I am the bitter wind howling and moaning
as I whip the stones of ruined buildings.
I am the moonlight pouring my beached beams
of light onto the world.
I am the stars whizzing and dashing through the
endless sky twinkling on all.
I am the trembling volcano's bubbling and boiling
as I mix my fiery brew.
I am the fluffy clouds dreamily floating through
the peaceful sky.
I am the night sky draping my huge silky
cloak far over the earth.
I am the earth bringing new life and new beginning
wherever I go.
I am the stones of the moors and valleys solemn
guardians to the end of time.
I am the ocean sparkling and flashing as I
play forever a youth.
I am fire spreading my blanket of flame wherever
my wicked journey takes me.
I am the mountains majestic and proud, fair
and joyful yet cruel and pitiless.
I am the sound of a new born baby crying
bringing hope and joy to our unstable future.

Wish I Was There!
Pat Heppel

The lazy Ionian Sea chases itself onto the beach,
Each tiny rippling wave spraying
Into thousands of rainbow, sparkling droplets
To bathe the smooth, glistening pebbles underfoot.
The turquoise bay semi-circles gently,
Sentinelled on either side by high promontories
Whose backs have borne the growth
Of olives, cypress and lemons for myriad years.

The sun, resplendent in its blazing, golden ring,
Bathes the sea in liquid gold.
At peace in this segment of high-domed sky,
It risks not the mask of invading clouds.
Unhindered, it shines forth, warming sea and sand,
Ripening fruits, bronzing bodies
And fulfilling its God-given task
To soak the land in nurturing light.

Far out, islands float in the azure sea
As if jettisoned there by long-ago civilisations,
And contented fishermen while away the day in boats
Which have seen many idyllic sunsets
Before their return to shore with nets
Brimming with slithery, silver fish,
Which will grace many a Grecian table
Alongside pasta, wine and crusty home-made bread.

Overhead, white, feathery jet-streams
Criss-cross the pale-blue velvet October sky.
The last holiday-makers of the year jetting in
To sample the delights of this jewelled isle.
Then, these tanned, swarthy people
Will jealously treasure their island paradise again,
Whiling away the mild, sunny winter
In trivial pursuits within their little white-washed homes.

Otter's Bay
Carole House

Over Otter's Bay gulls soar
on wings whiter than the silver sheen
of moonlight dancing on the palest shore.
In the shallows a heron stands aloof
and frozen for one still moment
balanced on its own reflection.

Where ocean and land meet and mingle
an armada of ducklings securely feed
within the harbour of their parents care,
while waves throw shawls of lacy foam
on silver filigrees of cobweb shore.

Over baked land storm clouds gather.
The first sharp shower of summer rain
machine-guns down upon the roof,
releasing the sweet scent of thirsty earth
as the sun dips its fiery gold while
cradled in the arms of cooling air.

Footsteps here remain undisturbed
until the last wave cobbles shell-mosaic
of seaform on the damp, dark sand.

This place makes gifts
without a single word.
Here we live our dreams.

Horizons Of My Youth
Andrew Frolish

Strange that I just remember it in summer.
Blinded by the ferocity of happiness
And the gleaming smiles of children.
Our hearts were airborne on currents of wonder
And an unmistakable sincerity that this would never end.

I believe those summers were truly longer
And everything that mattered was in our hands.
We tasted the sunshine and found it perfect.
The unbreakable circle, the familiar sounds
Fuelled the energy we spent unchecked.

The buildings eased into us with sublime grace,
And I was unaware it even happened until just yesterday.
The horizon spelled our world, and we were
Happy with its proximity. That treasured timeless
Place shaped and became the man you see.

Yesterday I stood on the playground and sensed that
Other time. I was surprised as it melted out of me
And made me drunk with recollection.
Surprised that I had preserved it so carefully, faithfully.
Surprised that I could will it back without concern.

So long ago, but now whenever I choose.
An eternity to become what we have become.
And though we each disappear one by one,
It is clear that the summers will never leave us -
Echoes and ghosts will murmur within us forever.

Winter In London- Or A Brave Attempt At Clarification By Confusion
Roger Plowden

The stored warmth of summer
Is in the Underground,
And the tomato plants are burgeoning
Inside the little signal-box
At Hyde Park corner.

So it was that in the coldest days
Of ideological struggle some men knew
From the financial peccadilloes of radical politicians
That the seeds of human frailty
Were stirring towards that summer
Of absolute inequality and individual profit.

December 1986

Bully Hill
Rhod Bevan

It's still
Here now
On this hill
And our stone
Where time ebbs as ever
At our mother Australia
And bows to the waterholes
Just like tears for Freya
Rusting her sinking over irons of the railyard
In the carmine cum-Eden's of New South Wales

It's still
Here now
On the blown leaves, love
Where the fat hill remembers
The one who could sing me
Up here with her sun
And who's Agena girl was she
Before the thunderstorms burst over irons of the railyard
And washed all the diamonds out of New South Wales

Love Is The Place
Suzy Clarke

Incubating in the cave of dreams

Is where I want to be.

Sojourn in another lust.

Voyeuristic obsession with Rapunzale's strung-out sister.

Sugar smash

Six hours short;

Middle-c love sonnets

For the souvenir idiot

That I am.

Cocktail sunset over our velvet crush goodbye.

Worth living here

In bittersweet love-cheat town.

The Derelict Mill
David J C Wheeler

In a wood up the lane
    stand the old, broken teeth
Which once were a mill's indestructible walls.
And the skeleton, gaunt
    in its blood daub of rust,
Of a wheel over which only rainwater falls,
With railings corroded,
    paths fast sealed by thorns,
And stories of ghosts in its echoing halls,
There's none but the hardy
    will still seek it out,
For something about these old ruins appals,
That somewhere so vital
    should die, repels most,
'Til only the poet or artist it calls.

Yet has nature re-clothed
    what we humans discard,
With multi-hued cloth of a rich, living green,
Whose tendrils reach up,
    glad to find firm support,
On which they, in their frailty, can fasten and lean,
So a cascade anew
    flashes white from the wheel,
Where the beautiful blooms of the bindweed are seen,
Which, despised 'though it is
    as a troublesome weed,
From abandonment's squalor this lost place would wean,
Set a seal on the kiss
    which transforms once again,
This derelict wraith by eternity's sheen.

Seven Days At Portreath
Ken Marshall

The tang of tallowed ropes
Coiled on a quayside.
The rhythmic murmuring
Of sea washed pebbles.
Picnicking with our hamper
On sultry afternoons - trying
To keep the Chardonnay cool!
Then lying side by side, watching
Cotton-bud clouds lazily chasing each other
High above the tips of the tall grass.
I remember your white lace so vivid
Against the green,
And that butterfly! - the one that
Nestled and was caught, mesmerised, as I was
By the gentle fragrance of your hair.

So many memories, so bittersweet.
We held hands,
And made the bracken crack!
As we ran up the rise,
Under melancholy cries, of seagulls.
Then, at the top, a clear view
Right across the cove
And inland to the village.
We could just see 'The Copper Kettle Inn'.
Did you know I went there, last year?
But, I won't go again.

It really could have worked you know,
If things had been different.

Sempre Venezia
Margaret Franklin

Lacking a man I love a city,
flexing erotic muscle
in its androgynous, aquatic,
labyrinthine ways.

The smiling facade welcomes me
each precious time we meet.
Through erogenous arches
I probe the secret places,
warm, damp,
gardens demurely hidden.

Others lay claim
but their adulterous lusts
melt into shadows
while our two pulses throb
with every coming together.

Serene, rapt, distinguished,
my city is so old
that I feel ever young again,
my soul sweetly sold.

I weep on taking leave
(like any grand affair),
breathing passionate promise
to return. The greatest consolation?
Unlike a blooded lover
my city will be there
for my eternity.

2 Weeks In March
Kevin Rolfe

Came from your wheezing bedside
Wishing to stay,
Got home late
In 2 minds,
And 1 state;
Cleaned and fixed the oven fan
For something to do
To remove the sterile ward
And the slow pain on view;
If I lost you
I'd lose my mind,
If you lost me
Would it not be before time?
Something removed
You'd already forgot.

City Of London Tree
Mark Kobayashi-Hillary

Ignored;
Posturing grandly.
Limp, leaves choke on;
      Daily smog.

Life in strange places.
      Defiant of reason.

Challenging cars,
The road,
      The surrounding noise,
         The people.

Bifurcation within a West One street.
Standing wise.

Lakeland
D C J Jones

April, Lakeland clear and crisp.
Above, blue skies with clouds like cottonwool twists
A long thin arrow of white mist
Hangs over Derwentwater Lake.

Helvelyn still majestic in winter's white
Stands high above the peaks - an awesome sight.
What beauty, so clean, so quiet, yet bright,
But with such power and inner fight
For those who venture to match its might.

A gentle breeze unfurls, the mist it drifts away,
The mountain now a clear reflection in the still waters lake.
The Cat-bells opposite shimmers. Its spring colours
Change as the puffs of cloud pass over.
What a gentle but glorious scene
A morning - what a dream.

*Cat-bells = Large Hill/Mountain

Christmas In Monterey
Margaret Paroutaud

No winter cold
But white and shining with
Soft mist like Angora fur,
Like swansdown on the hills.
Still He is born
And all the beasts bow down
On Christmas night;
On all the ranches
In the valley they remember
The hour of His birth.
Fishermen marvel
At the miracle
Of their nets;
Gleaming silver of fish.
And now the drying seine
Draped like grey cable -
Knitting on the walks.
He Guilio, che bella sorpresa!
He is born.

Haga Haga Beach, S Africa
A Very Special Place
   Jane Finlayson

Shredded sunlight sifting on honey gold sand,
Halcyon pools, rock-rimmed, topaz-tanned-
Wild plume, spray spume,
From the crinkled, silvering sea.

Sunlight, eye-bright, high-light, sky-light,
clouds pearl, unfurl, eddies swirl, clouds pearl,
Above the wrinkled, whispering sea.

Wave-beat, heart-beat, minute traces
Of minuscule feet -
Snail trail, crab claw,
Opaline shells scatter the shore -
Waves break, heart-ache, angel fish, sea snake -
Horseshoe beach, green-feathered strand,
Seagulls scour the glistening land.

My Garden
Rose Horscroft

My garden is a special place
Where I wander back in time
As I sit dreamily in the sun
With my grandson's hand in mine
The scent of the geraniums
The buzzing of a bee
The faithful eyes of my Rottie
With his chin upon my knee
It is so peaceful sitting here
It seems that time stands still
This garden's full of memories
That I recall at will
I remember my children playing
With daisies in their hair
And now their children do the same
They never have a care
There was my Robin who always came
Indeed he was so very tame
He would always be so near to me
We developed an affinity
The years go by and he still comes
To gaze at me and wait for crumbs
Could another be so bold?
Or perhaps like me he's getting old
I gaze at the beautiful shady trees
A view that's always sure to please
I feel contented sitting here
I love it any time of year
I wake my grandson, kiss his brow
I think we'd better go in now
The sun has gone, the squirrel runs
I can't wait until tomorrow comes
The lilac blooms, the cherries harden
And I'll find solace in my garden

Woodland Wonderland
Alan Taylor

Long grass waving in the summer air,
A fragile green for the valley to wear.
With dappled shade from trees so tall,
'Twas a wonderland I well recall.

The stream that trickled through its bed
Ran down into the lake, and fed
Fishes placid in the reeds
God's hand supplying all their needs.

That path I walked in childhood days,
Basking in the sun's warm rays,
With father, mother, sister, gran,
Was surely part of God's great plan.

But then we had to homeward wend
Back to London's dim East-end.
We laid to rest in shelter deep
Each night the din frustrating sleep.

The outside world was burning bright
As bombs exploded in the night.
Tracer shells explored the sky,
Seeking out those planes on high.

My siren suit was warm and snug
My mother calm with kiss and hug.
Yet how I longed for valley, lake,
And sun and shade, as I lay awake.

Some mortals must, against God's plan
Scheme to kill another man
Because he has a diverse view
Be it Catholic, Protestant or Jew.

Let witless wonders waging wars,
Who in God's name go breaking laws,
Leave those of peace and love to find
Their special place within mankind.

Wild Camp Dawn
Dominic Carr

Winds blow through the ruddy
Skies of dawns reverie
The earth is crisp and fresh
The sky steel cold and gold
My reflection in the mountain lake
Looks old.
Is this the same boy that
Once looked back at me?
Here, in this early morning
Slept - rough ageness -
Old hands.
Waves filled with silver light
Lap at the shore.
Mornings orchestra warms up
Waiting for the conductor
To come to the podium
With wild resplendent golden hair
To conduct the day.

Summer And Winter
Jeff Hancocks

Far distant shore and hills beyond of ancient keeping,
What secrets now you shade within your bowels;
What tears, what joys, what lovers knew your treasures;
Yet even now you stand content, beneath the skies.

The skies with myriad, sparkling diamonds,
Each one holds a kiss, a lovers pledge;
Yet 'ere before the morning sky awakens,
The stars that lit those eyes, lie deep in shroud.

The trickling sands, from palms so gently flowing,
Each grain, the purity of unspoiled youth,
But darkening tide then turns, and starts its ebbing,
It takes its thrill and leaves its waste to mar.

The rough and rocky slopes hold regal beauty,
And even beds of bliss are offered there,
Now, pleasures lost, the years and ages lengthen,
As others steal your breathless visions shared.

Oh to be content again, beneath the surface,
To know once more, a glow of inner warmth,
To leave the icy cold of howling winters,
And share the dawn of new life giving spring.

But even summer has no place for all who enter
Onto life's revolving, restless stage,
So autumn days please lend your sunset,
And bring a peace of mind, to evening's days.

Paradise
Graham John

My childhood's extra special place,
a narrow gorge where nature still
resists man's headlong greedy race.

A stream, in summer, a gentle rill
which wanders gently in the vale
accompanied by a songbird's trill.

In winter, deep beneath the gale
the river swells and roars with rage
to make denuded trees look frail.

This is nature's glorious stage.
Her vegetation in bright array,
has stood the test of time and age.

When I was young, I loved to stray
amid the trees and bushes there.
This was where I longed to play.

To explore and sniff the air.
To find the tiny waterfalls
God, in His wisdom, let me share.

Asir

Carol Fisher

Metamorphic mountains of indisputable majesty
zigzag jagged peaks celestial soar
as Earthbound thunder rills descending
with precipitating torrents roar.

Arid baked wadis with solar bleached tread
embrace ephemeral streams surge-anarchy bound
devouring the tessellating desiccated plain
with rumbling, booming, rending sound

Boulder entrainment of once granitic grain
as circumscribed lava escapes unprotesting
a colloid of wonder, liquid delight
tearing its parameters retainers detesting

Provocative meanders entrance the rhythmic flow
as tantalising velocities segregate the load
with splendid synchronocity to aggravate, alleviate
the mingling of saline and fresh sediment erode.

*The Asir is part of the Red Sea escarpment on the Western Saudi
Arabian Shield and formed as a result of tectonic activity millions
of years ago.*

Madingley
American War Cemetery
David Sampson

Lashing rain washes the stain it creates
From Christian crosses and Jewish stars.
Sentry still they stand at attention;
On green pastures like white ghostly sheep.
Gathered row upon row shepherd penned;
Obedient to their anthems call.

Young men not knowing a heroes duty,
Or caring even, but doing it;
Adventured to deaths' door.
Down the stone paths reflective puddles
Gather the rain that sheets down, yet fails
To erase the graffiti message;
In a neighbouring town. *Yanks Go Home.*

Lakeside Memories
Margaret Gannon

As I sit here alone, the sun on my face
this remote faraway lakeside
was our hideaway place

Remember the times we sat here and laughed
the long grass obscuring silhouettes that passed

It was here that you held me, you told me you cared
such precious warm moments with the lakeside we shared

The sweet smell of bluebells form memories of bliss
it was here that you stole our very first kiss

I come here alone now as time has passed by
sometimes to remember, sometimes to cry
the lakeside so tranquil, it glistens like gold
what loving old memories this lakeside must hold.

A Mother's Arms
Nicola Pym

These fragile, padded walls
will soon fall and shatter
my warmth and comfort
will soon release me into a harsh, cruel sphere.

These padded walls can no longer protect me
I can at any moment fall from Nirvana, with a
bang
I hit reality
my padded walls, pick me up
and encase me once more.

Mi Bonita Latina
John Dewar

Senorita do you dance alone
Across La Plaza de Espana?
And do the old flamenco songs
Beat gypsy rhythms in your soul?
Do you forget about the cold days
In Sevilla's warm September breeze?
Do you lose yourself in Calle Betis
Among friends and scented orange trees?

Maria, I try to find you
In my dreams and in my heart
I am with you in Andalusia
And not two worlds apart.

Senorita I must tell you
Your smile gives everything to me.
Your strength and your passion
Has set my spirit free.

Senorita you do not see me
As I dance this dance alone.
Mi Bonita Latina de Sevilla
Will never take me home.
But though I may never be there
I know what I would see there.
I will always find my Spanish skies
In sweet Maria's eyes.

Enamorado

Edinburgh Military Tattoo
Kathleen Y Ambler

That night it was clammy when dusk fell
And crowds made their way to their seats.
And then it had all began happening,
An event which just cannot be beat:

The pipes and drums there they assembled
All clad with their tartan display,
And the breeze started just gently blowing
And the crowd just got carried away.

And tunes were so carefully chosen
As the pipers played stood side-by-side,
And yes: I'm so glad to be Scottish
For this moment just fills me with pride.

The beat of the drums and my heartbeat
Are just beating together in tune,
And no, there's no roof up above me,
Just God's sky and the light of the moon.

The gifts God has granted those people
Are quite awesome, and to say the least.
So I'll say Thank You, God, for this moment
As my eyes watch the end of this feast.

'Haste Ye Back', all those from foreign countries
And again we'll unite as just one:
Who could think that a Military Tattoo
Can unite all the world into one.

My Foreign Country
Aileen E Graham

Open the creaking oaken door
To a land of remembered joy.
Step under the wooden perfumed arch
To a green growing land
Of lovingly tended Nature.
Experience anew the wond'rous encounter
With a strange house made of glass
Home to a profusion of yellow tomatoes
Passed from a Grandpa's proffered hand
Into the eager clutches of a child.
Envisage my excitement and anticipation
In preparation for this annual visit
To Grandpa's country garden paradise –
As foreign a country
To me –
A tenement child of the fifties
As Africa is –
To my child of today.

Arranmore
Kathleen Brady

When I walk the roads of Arranmore
And daily there I roam,
I'm filled with joy as I meet each friend,
And they say 'You're welcome home'

For many years I stayed away,
And I wonder now just why,
Because these days it breaks my heart
When I have to say goodbye.

What is it about Donegal
That draws me to it so?
But the longing for it's in my heart
No matter where I go.

They say God placed a bit of heaven,
Just off the Rosses shore,
And I've no doubt it's 'Heaven on Earth',
This Isle of Arranmore

I'm proud that my ancestors
Trod these same roads as I,
I think their spirits call to me,
In the wind I hear them sigh

'Come back again to Arranmore'
Soft voices to me call,
'And live the life God's given you,
Home here in Donegal'.

Caitlin Ni Ruadhrui

On Travelling Through The Hautes-Alpes
Barry Jones

I will sing a hymn to the mountains,
I will rejoice in their majesty and splendour
I am awed in their presence,
In their innate power and might.

This is my prayer to the mountains,
This is my homage to their silent serenity,
I am humbled by their steadfastness,
By their granite-sure foundation.

My heart aspires to the mountains,
My soul yearns for their spiritual balm,
I am willing to follow their paths ever upward
Into the very ways of God.

I will lift up my eyes to the mountains,
I will forever abide in their snow-calm peaks,
My spirit resides in the mountains,
In their enduring solace and peace.

Midsummer
Geoff Hockley

In the hot noontide haze
Green grassy stems, crowned with rainbow seed
Marching in tune to the cricket's trill
She walked from between the circle stones
Flowers caressed her feet
The sun behind glowed through gold gauze
Raven hair, silver white skin
She gazed about her, curious
A stranger in this land
Would she permit!
Could I guide her?
For how long would she stay?
Or would I with her
This honeysuckle scented midsummer night
In moon-glow, dark piled clouds in light sky
Return through the ring of stone?
The gateway to her world
To be with her here or there,
Or would I be alone?

The Resting Place
J D Williams

Where time has moulded walls of marbled sequence,
The generations of souls that walk
Endlessly through pillars of darkness have been lit
As if by some celestial fire.

Why, here even the very stone seems live to beauty,
Where coloured shadows of a summer sun
Dapple the memory filled slabs.

Tokens of dear remembrance and loved-filled tears,
Anxious not to grieve yet full of remorse
At things too late encountered,
Drop slowly between bare feet, alone yet not alone.

The hopeful sigh, the reproaching gesture,
The high piping reeds as they enrequiem those beloved,
And even those unbeloved,
All cherish hope,
While Faith, like an ever-climbing paradisal bird,
Rises above all, covers all, enhances all
With the breath of Life.

Sheering Sunday 1920s
H Marfleet

The Rector blessed them in his benediction,
His Sunday suppliants murmured their assent,
A private prayer, they slowly made their way then,
Amply renewed with holy nourishment.

The gentry's Rolls swept them away to luncheon,
The farmer's Fords to solid farmhouse fare,
The labourers ambled to their pint of ale,
Then home to what their meagre purse might bear.

As favoured armchairs claimed work-weary bones,
The village, hushed then, slumbered at its rest,
And week-long labour shut wind-weathered eyes,
As drooping heads with healing sleep were blest.

Soon steaming kettles sang their merry measures,
While mantle clocks chimed out the time for tea,
Sleep-stiffened limbs revived and slowly stirred,
As liquid amber worked its sorcery.

Ere long the bidding bell of evensong,
Issued its summons through the dusking air,
As waning day, with but few hours to gift,
Called forth, once more, the faithful to their prayer.

Slowly the darkening shades of evening fell,
As lighted lamps bewitched the flighting moth,
And village elders reminisced their youth,
While youth embraced, and shyly pledged their troth.

The gifted hours fast faded into night,
To wait their appointed span ere they returned,
A new dawn beckoned in the new day's toil,
Marking the end of rest so richly earned.

The sun rose on the gentry's heritage,
The gentry rose to breakfast on the lawn,
The working farmers raised their eyes to heaven,
And blest the day that labourers were born.

And so each trod the path that he knew best,
Each to his own and his intended place;
Gentry and working farmers, labourers all,
The epitome of Britain's Island Race.

Prague
John A Davis

Necromantic city in which
Like conspirators shadows foregather
As at twilight the alchemist sun
Turns the leaden Vltava to gold

Over the tumbled graveyard
- All that is left of the ghetto -
A bat from the ivy-draped elders
Draws arabesques in the dusk

Down a dimly lit alley
Footsteps sound on the cobbles
But the doors are shut against strangers
And the windows stare out with glazed eyes

The puppet apostles strut past
As the clock in the market strikes twelve
To prevent his constructing another
The master who made if was blinded

The menacing murmur of bells
Tolls for Protestant, Jesuit, Jew
The magicians were hung in iron cages
When they asked to walk out in the sun

I gaze at a carving of Christ
He stares back again with a look
That tells me more than I wanted
To know how He felt on the cross.

The Moor And David
Archibald Gorman

He is the moor's topography,
its pools and burns and reservoirs,
its marsh and heather-hardened skies.
And down the dank Auchmountain Glen
he'd scatter Whinhill sparks at dusk
and often bring quaint creatures home,
(Flint Mill Lane menagerie),
only to release them after
spells of frantic circumscription.
He'd baffle trout and pike with skills
fine-tuned on solitary days
spent high above the fretting town
and also garner golf balls sliced
adeptly into dam and whin,
the mangled ones anatomised,
their inner lives exposed to eyes
still fascinated, unblas.

(But water is his instrument,
he plays across its surfaces
his sad mnemonic variations).

Safe In My Sanctuary Of Secrecy
David C Quenby

Each morning as the dawn breaks
and welcomes another day
I see my reflection in the window pane
     and wonder
      where am I going
    why do I live a life full of
   insecurity and false hope
    where is my utopia;

Another day is dawning
and so I don the mask of libertine
with gay abandon I meet the world
      no time
   to let me feelings show
or let my mask slip
to them I am the jester the butt of mockery
the fool who cannot feel the pain
   the misery of loneliness;

They do not understand
for they cannot understand
I do not blame them
     nor chastise them
   for they are ignorant of my truth
my sadness is for me to share with myself
my pain is inside, and must not show
   in case someone understands
     and shows me . . . pity
oh God! Then the remorse,
the sanctity of peace will be
    forever destroyed;

Let me brave another dawn
alone and frightened
yet safe in my sanctuary of secrecy
    knowing of my despair
        alone:

Rain

Jim Jefferies

Oh incarcerated in this desert land,
Wrought from arid mountains and burning sand.
I know the beauty of what the great men say
The poets of the latter day.
Blinded and bound with iron chain
I feel the magic of the summer rain.
Oh in England, in the breaking dawn
Leaves stir and mushroom spawn.
Cattle graze the silver sea
And the nightjar calls from a distant lea.
Like some crying spirit I tread these sacred grounds
To haunt the inn beyond the downs.
I call out to them, but they do not hear.
For I am of some distant time, some far off year.
Alas, the rain is no more than my tears
Grieving for the passing years.
I know I will die in this putrid sand,
A forgotten name in a forgotten land.

The Helm Wind
Carole Hanson

Hear the approaching roar and thunder
across the Pennines on Cross Fell.
Comes the Helm wind mad and bullying
to the place once known as 'Fiends Fell'
till St Augustine held a mass.
Erecting a cross upon the grass.

With the Vale of Eden down below
blanketed by swirling mists.
This plunderer of nature calls without
respect for grass or crops.
Uprooting trees along its route and all
around frost-shattered rocks.

Knocking stones right out of walls,
this untamed Helm Wind fights and brawls
with everything along its path.
Blowing beaks off geese as well.
Nothing here escapes its wrath.

A strong, marauding enemy.
A foe to fear on old Cross Fell.
As breeding dotterels pair in love,
broad-winged buzzards wheel tirelessly above
where reindeers in far off days ate white-
flowered cloudberry whilst they grazed.

Be warned all you who walk the Fell.
The Helm Wind has a tale to tell.
As nature bows before its master, the
Helm Wind brings its own disaster.

The House
P H Thomas

In a sea of uncut grass,
the For Sale sign lists drunkenly,
bent by the force of a winter storm.
The house is empty now, almost derelict,
its occupants dead and gone.
How will it know it's Christmas?
There is no one to hang the trimmings,
or decorate the tree.
Through the window, I think I see
Gossamer grey ghosts of yesteryear,
laughing and happy,
seated amidst a mountain of food.
The image fades,
my mind saw what it wanted to see.
Nothing remains,
only memories embedded deeply within its walls.
The house, in its deathly silence,
weeps with me for Christmas past.

Formalutz (Mallorca)
V Weston

Walking up the narrow lane from Sollar
with its fine stone houses and courtyard gardens
through the valley of the orange and lemon groves
trees laden with fruit, air heady with fragrance
in warm sunshine mid January with the high
Serra de Tramuntana as backdrop,
mountain tops half concealed in mist;
following up alongside the flowing stream
to where lies the hill village of
Formalutz, amid olive, pine, cypress
and flowering almond trees

Narrow lanes, steps and alleys
invite in all directions
and terraced restaurants
overlook the view
which changes every moment
in grandeur

There at the restaurant of 'The Bull'
fresh squeezed oranges, olives from the terraces
bread newly baked, a
special sacramental meal
in a paradisal place

The Spinney Cherryhinton
Janet Cullup

A wooden stile bars the gap
I ran through as a child
Into the soft lush green
From the grey concrete
Of my home in Romsey Town.

A magical place
Enchanting imagination
With a living fountain of nature
That sustains in middle age.

Shy violets and sun-bright aconite's,
Wild cherries, rose hips and the weird,
Mysterious, old man's beard.
Carved in the chalk face
Of an overgrown quarry ~ slides,
Shady trees to climb or picnic beside.
Shaggy bushes, hiding places, dens.

I close my eyes and smell again
Swelling green moss damp with rain
Hear the swish of waving grass
Shouts of voices from the past.

Feel the sharp sting of a nettle.
Life's lessons ~ experience.
Innocence surrounded by danger,
Perfection preserved by memory
Existing still ~ yet different.

As a child I savoured freedom,
Uninhibited by the shadows
Deviant abusers cast.
Wild brambles tore my knees
But not my heart.

I weep for children today
Protected by ever watchful eyes.
Unable to escape, be themselves,
Ride the rainbow of creation
In union with nature.

Plants grown in shadows
Can never be as strong
As those lifting their faces
Unhindered to the sun.

Dering Wood
Margaret Wheatley

A distant vista -
all mysterious and magical,
dappled sunlight casting shadows.

The quiet echo -
so penetrating yet velvety,
scented 'main rides' leading beyond.

In childhood wonder -
rich rhododendrons so stately,
purpled 'mountains' reaching skywards.

Those ancient pathways -
some meandering in secrecy,
throbbing birdsong wafting above.

Such golden moments -
yes remembering a nightingall,
ardent unique thrilling high notes.

Now decades later -
new generations quite happily,
nurture rebirth giving beauty.

This woodland alive -
rare tranquillity, our heritage,
breathing wild life, spreading clearly.

Heart Of The City
Deborah Whyte

At the metropolis of me
there was once a nucleus
it flinched within-
o dutiful device.
It flushed lifeblood,
a colourless solution
through thin arctic arms.
How anaemic you were,
until

A neonatal seed nestled in your heart.
It cultivated and coaxed
it filled you with flesh
dear timepiece of red.
You murmured and ticked
despite this mad metropolis.
For a celestial wine elated you,
its warmth bubbled
through your hands `- so nourishing.
Now you grow kernel with the feelings within me
Subsisting always on his love.

For Mark

Beachcombing
Samantha Chadda

With flags and windmills I claimed this land
and on it built my home.
Every fort, every castle, dam and waterway of childhood,
moulded by youthful hope,
studded with the pebble armour of innocence,
and glistening with emerald weed tendrils
of childish exuberance.
Waves run up the shore to meet me, greeting waves,
my long ago friends of endless summer mornings
in that Sunshine Corner -
digging for Jesus and singing for joy of life
and of this place - my place in the world.
Foamy fingers tickle my soles and drag back
sandy layers of conscience, to reveal my forgotten self;
of towel-wrapped shivering shoulders,
and burnished skin streaked with salty traces of adventure.
That watery fluid light surrounding,
fills the shaft of memory to illuminate my truth,
and at the water's edge, I am again gathering
the pink and coral-bellied treasures of childhood.

Enchanted
Rita Pal

Forests of desire thorned
With drenched bewildered passions,
Sequenced contoured twilights
Streamed for silent dreams,
Laced in softened kisses
Strewn with rose petal caresses

Your oceaned eyes drown me
Trials and tricks for my soul,
Fragments for my mind
In deliriums of madness
In frantic search for immortal love.

Replenishing banished exiles
With enchanting words,
Enticing visions,
Enlightening charms,
Embrace my secret love
 For all the valleys of time.

Hong Kong 1976
Angela Cheyne

Its name was Aberdeen
the other side of Fragrant Harbour
an inlet of Hong Kong.

50 metres from the shore,
a universe of neon twinkling
stark against the purple sky:
the floating restaurants that bob
and sway against the briny tide.

The paddled barges
that ply their way
from shore to opulent haven,
there to disgorge those gourmets
eager for the good smells and
bon homie that await the
laden purse.

A shadow in the wake of flecked
lights on rippled water;
a meagre boat with a sleeping child
the mother at the helm;
the tang of salt and putrid fish
that lap the nostrils
like a mucus
run dry.

To eke a living plying to and forth
between the land and off-shore
cornucopia,
to vye for custom for a coin
this is an existence
in Aberdeen,
the other side of Fragrant Harbour
an inlet of Hong Kong.

Wensleydale On A Hot Summer's Day
Gerald Conyngham

Rivers   meander   sluggishly
Across a brown scorched landscape,
Past fields divided by old stone walls
Painstakingly erected.

A sense of prayer and worship
Within the ruined abbeys;
Castles overlook
                 the villages,
Built to repel attackers . . . and keep in dissidents.

Old market towns
Their   wide   open   streets and ancient churches
And spacious squares alive with people.

Flowers everywhere
         Hang in their baskets
                 Like offerings to the sun

    Vast open valleys,
Eroded millions of years ago
    By U-shaped glaciers
Forcing their way through.

This place   this   time   this   emptiness
Framed visions of eternity
Fleetingly seen and felt.

Cemetery Junction
R P Avery

A haven of peace beside
a main road whose traffic
hurtles towards
an early grave.

I sit alone with my thoughts
a solitary figure
among the statues
and the stones
of long forgotten souls.

Their silence engulfs me
seeping into my conscience
subtly soothing away
the aches of eternity.

Their rest
rests me
their calmness
calms me
the sun
burns me
before the road
chokes me.

And as my mind unwinds
too soon it's time
to leave my haven of peace
beside a main road.

The Church-What Is It ?
Anne Gray

I travelled towards Lincoln
And what did I espy?
A glorious, grandiose building
Just nestling in the sky
For some, this lovely building,
In all its majesty,
Its beauty and its splendour
Their Church would seem to be

My thoughts were greatly stirred then
And questions came to me
What really is the true Church
Whatever can it be?
I thought of all the buildings
Where people meet to pray
To worship, to praise our Lord
Just buildings one might say.

I thought then of the people
With individual needs
Bringing these to God in prayer
On His great love to feed.
And then I thought of many
Who bring their joys to share
So all can feed on blessing
And for each other care

What to you is Church, my friends?
The people or the place?
All those who come together
To find our Saviour's Grace?
The building where they gather
Or folk who gather there?
It really is important
To know, and then to share

The church to me is people
Who showed me that they care,
For there, within that building
The love of God they shared.
let us each be God's true Church
And to the world display
The precious Love of God to all
Yes, each and every day.

Marloes

N Voake

Smaller than pinheads in the fissured rock
Sea snails clung, like scattered seeds
Shaken from some universal consciousness;
My spirit slid with theirs into the stone
And felt the power of sun and sea
While, in that time, I glimpsed
A world I had not seen before;
Their minute shells were formed of rock
Yet still they shared with me their living flesh;
But I must leave them long before the weather breaks
And rolling waves threaten their rocky home.
Perhaps, when winter comes,
I too will feel the sea
That foams around that lonely rock
Two hundred miles away

Heather's Pool
Pamela Gott

I float, balanced and buoyed by water,
on netways of rainbow loops, meshes of sunlit rings.
A light wind makes the tall hornbeam hedge move silently,
mottled with flickering movement underneath
as the sun throws light and shadows from the water on the leaves
above the looped blue water where the swallows dive
and sip in seconds as they dip and flash
and leave for a moment small concentric rings.
    I lie in the sun on brown-baked prickle-grass
and feel the tickle of water drying on my skin
and trickles of water dripping from wet hair.
    The thistledown drifts down, turning to run across the surface,
takes off again to float like silvered stars,
or, captured and held by little waves, sinks damply down
to join the grass-stems and small beetles, or floats
for a while, a fragile island for insects
- clamber waterlogged aboard or drown.
    The water a second time feels colder still
on sun-warm legs and arms,
splits in light-splintered fragments on the surface,
while below I swim from cold blue patch to warm,
from the dark shadow of the cone-shaped cypresses
and float with the stretched blue sky suspended above
blue as the water below.

N N N N
Cath Simpkins

9 30 am.
New Year's Day.
1998.
Knavesmire Racecourse, York.

Frost being melted
by the sun
on my back
and
I take a photograph -
a self portrait
that shows a Daliesque giraffe
but only on fire from the inside.
Upright, a needle for Cleopatra,
but sun plays strange tricks on light
and
my circus stiltwalker's appearance is only an illusion.

but with these legs of umbra and penumbra
and my seven league boots,
I can attain many miles and miles away from my roots
and be
the New Year, New me.

Into The Unknown
Gwyneth E Scott

I am going away so bid me adieu
Far from familiar surroundings to pastures new
And I know not what awaits me at the other end
But I pray there I shall find a friend -
A helping hand to guide me through
The hours of darkness - my faith to renew.
Though my mind is filled with despair
Go I must to shed all care.
I have reached the cross-roads - there is no turning back
My weary footsteps urge me forward along the well-beaten track.
The wheels of progress are whirling round
It is now out of my hands - help I have found.
So who am I to turn away
From those who will guide me along life's way?
To bring me back from the shadows into light.
Once more to face the future with courage and might.
And so I must tread what is to me the unknown road
As I have lingered too long - heavy is my load.
My body is weary and my heart is cold
So stretch forth your comforting arms
And welcome me into the fold.

Autumn
Carole Luke

Thumbing through
stiff, cellophaned
photograph albums
I remember autumn
at Sycamore Avenue -

Brown keys whirred down
like busy helicopter blades,
chestnut globes
freed from green-spiked shells
thudded to the ground to drown

in leaves -
raw red, lemon yellow, copper,
kaleidoscope-coloured,
silting the house sides;
drifting through opened patio doors,

following the summer sun's last rays;
covering concrete slabs,
crazy-paved paths;
brushing my billowing washing;
the scurrying squirrel,

settling silently on the earth,
a rustling blanket for insects;
tumbling, sprawling games for my sons,
galoshes shuffling, scuffing,
sloshing through mouldering mounds -

placed in piles for bonfire burning.

Arran

Andrew R Stumpf

Glenashdale Falls; Glen Sannox' tree;
Mealach's Grave and that old dying oak.
Corries' pub and the wood carvers' hut.
Goatfell and dark pine pathways
Behind a boulder hidden in a stream.

Its lost some of its beauty I thought;
And gazing in memories,
Wondered in my gaze,
What I really sought.

For whatever I see ~in any land
~ There's something there before;
Before my sight ~ a thought!
The place or me ~ what has changed?
But I can't lock her sight away
~ as Everyone says I ought.

The price we pay for our mistakes
Can be greater than the sin.
And will I ever pay the cost?
Beauty once shared through two pairs of eyes.
~ But, Arran? Half its beauty, now, seems lost.

Candlelight And Prose
Siân Wallman

I am writing by candlelight.
There seems nothing better, or more fitting,
    at moments like these.

Others make use of this light.
That atmospheric mood enhancer,
    a conductive lover's illumination.

Instead I write words.
Words which move fast but reach nowhere,
    slow words travelling the globe.

Fastidiously searching corners.
For reason, meaning and common sense,
    in a place of confusion.

Words are a place in themselves.
A solitary spectre of security,
    protecting the writer from outer wilds.

Candlelight and prose.
An accompaniment of truth,
    where the joining equals a state of mind.

Words are a therapy.
The movement of hand, eye and pen,
    on susceptible paper.

Absorbency is the key.
So the words may reflect the mind,
    paper accepting scribbling pen.

I am writing by candlelight.
For no apparent reason,
    but liking the rhythm of life as it flows.

Hall Place, Bexley
Dorothy Ireland

The house is a marriage
Of Elizabethan brick and Jacobean chequer-board
Set within a courtyard
Of russet herringbone.
The leaded windows
Reflect the pleasing prospect
Of its garden walks,
Its rose-beds and fantastic topiary,
And the steps gently shelving
To the grassy verge of a stream.
But the stones are old
Older than the place . . .
And once owned Latin
For their mother-tongue.
Dismembered from an ancient Abbey
Miles away,
And brought here -
Betrayed into enemy hands -
For dressing the laity's
Unholy walls.
Time has been kind
To strange bed-fellows
Such as these.
The neutral elements
Have weathered down all evidence
Of old griefs . . . old factions
To one harmonious facade.
And within . . .
History has closed the page
At last.
It's all one now . . .
From the echo of a footfall
In the Minstrel Gallery
To the solitary shadow
On the stairs.

Hornsea Cliffs
G Slaney

The cold brown clay of Hornsea's coast
Is sculptured by the cruel north sea,
which heeds not critics of its work
nor matters what the season be.
Through winter's storms it hammers hard
removing slabs with utmost ease.
Then rolls them up and down the sand
and digests them in salty seas.
Between the tides I walk the beach
admiring curves and flats and splits,
and see a clump of farmland turf
as on some tower of clay it sits.
A fence which once did guard the edge,
now tumbled halfway down the scree.
Waiting there to journey forth
upon the unrelenting sea.
Where once a farm house proudly stood,
stand now an empty shell of stone.
The byres having long since gone.
In sorrow now it stands alone.
The hungry sea creeps forward still,
devouring all that man has built.
The sea a factory of its own
turning mankind's work to silt.
And yet I cannot but admire
natures own art gallery
built into Hornsea's brown clay cliffs
which proudly stand for all to see.

Two Places
Julian Dorr

You smelt fantastic and your eyes were dark.
Yellow heat, ploughed earth
and desire driving.
That green place; bank and bluebells,
shaded sweet soil,
where we embraced for the first time.
The only time I really remember.
Every emotion, every teenage ambition
collided in a moment
when, in a tangle of clothing and grass,
I touched another human soul.
And found my place in the picture.

Glendalough In Autumn
V M Cubitt

Wisps of mists that swirl and curl and drift on ripples of mire -
A bottomless well, a gentle swell of earth's bosom trapped in fire
Pan's pipes whisper in your ear - faint the tunes you want to hear
For, locked in the mud and endless time - is a tale I've yet to share .
Listen awhile and make sense of the scene -
These gentle hills wrapped warm in green -
And feel the air as with one caress - It drains away life's toil and
stress.
Where the silver birch lays down an arm dipping the water with
magic charm -
And playing with droplets, while overhead, the sky is studded with
lead.
The swifts swoop down, where angels tread - and all - is peace
A peace and calm. But in my head - a ditty, comes to mind -
Oh, Glendalough - Oh, Glendalough - I lost my heart to thee -
A million miles, nay, a million smiles - you're where I want to be -
A bewitching flute - plays a lilt, pretty and lithe and free -
Oh, Glendalough - Oh, Glendalough - do you ever think of me?
The autumn sky, speckled high - with flecks of frosted foam -
Beckon me - so in-vit-ing-ly - and fold the lake around -
And as I gaze upon its face I know my heart is lost -
Not to the youth of yesterday, but oh how great the cost -
To think that I - in all my dreams - never thought I'd be -
In Glendalough - In Glendalough - across the Irish Sea.-
And though I search - and searched some more -
I never found the one -
That told me tales of Irishmen - and how St Patrick won -
Upon the lakes green heather bank - I'd hum a mournful tune -
And let the love of country things, fade like the dew at noon . . .
The sun is setting, an orange sphere - and in the waters face -
I see another orb shining clear - with love entwined with grace -
And in the rustle of the trees I vow that every year -
I will return to Glendalough, to search beneath each shady rock -
The heart I left behind that day - deep beneath the open clay -
Buried with a tear of love - and a promise made to stay.

Portland
J A Coles

Umbilical cheisl strand gaunt rolling strident
holds at poor beast from breaking away
homes rise in tight curve and stutter the hill
then blanched carcass guards wounds
grey flanks of Portland hunger earth skin
torn hollowed Isle
beggars her way while others made king
passive despair invalidates dreams of cathedrals
cold comfort resides with light and shadow thin
barbed wire runs out entwined as brown weed
patrols lost missions amid rubble washed green
queen Anne's lace courts grave yard of Georgians and some
headstones lurch to ground of their gain
departed rest long on bed of white stone
and ever the sea mounting siege
expires thunder as mauled walls repulse
the old adversary

Hong Kong Handover Poem
Katherine Holmgren

The tears of the old colonials
fall in droves
as the *PLA take over the roads.
And as fireworks brightly lit the sky
   the gods and the people
        from heaven did cry.
Millions of dollars
went up in smoke
and the dragon god opened his mouth
                    and spoke.
For the dead of the past
from both sides
seem to agree
this is not a time
to look on with glee.
So all of them
let fall their tears
to mirror the earthly people's fears.

* Peoples Liberation Army

Fragments Of An Awakening
W E Hobson

At day's birth when the flailing sun appears
And we are locked within our warm cocoon
When all is quiet, all fears at rest
And thoughts transcend the fantasy of dreams
Then is the hour of thinking blessed
When reawakened hopes emerge
Slanting like birds in the Spring sky
From the rough beauty of each nest.

The moment has a perfect liquid joy
Condensed from longing streaming in the blood
The morning stirs our new awareness
Recreated, sensitivity poised
Twixt frail delirium and sensuousness
Those friendly harbingers of day
That haunt the yet unwakened hour
With gently touching warm finesse.

The morning grows intransigently pure
And we encompassed in that time
Know all our thoughts will turn and twist,
Like tides draw near and then recede
As if to some primeval tryst
When dreams and hopes then newly spun
Sun-blessed, unreal, and web like cling
Will vanish with the morning mist.

You Searching For You
Basia Palka

You will not find yourself
at your local pub
at the cinema
or at a French cafe
not in a railway station
or airport lounge
not at the checkout queue as you stand
neither at mother's over Sunday lunch
not at the single's club
or the jazz festival in Nairn
not in your living room
where you thought you just might
not over a stove
dinner for fine friends again
not on the telephone when nothing is said
nor through letters when quotes are written
or at a news vendor's stand
not in the paper
where you thought you'll find news of some kind
not in a book - intellectual food
certainly not at the ice-cream van
not in church
or at a meditation weekend abroad
nor on the streets of New York
you're either found
or you're not -
it's not a geographical point
of any sort

Imagine
Karen Muir

Hills and mountains stretching for miles,
Covered in seas of purple heather.
Listen to the sounds of the Highlands,
The rushing of the rivers,
The cries of the hawks,
The echoes of ghosts of battles won and lost.
Castles and ruins of ages past,
Custodians of a land seeped in the
Blood, sweat and tears of many.
Towns and villages caught in timeless beauty,
Nestled in such breathtaking surroundings.

Pride inbred in nations old and new,
Full of love and dignity.
Listen to the sounds of these lands,
The cries for understanding,
The beseeching for compassion,
The pounding of the oceans on history's rocks.
Lochs and lakes which predate man,
Overseers of secrets and lore
Of a land which pervades the very soul.
The mountainous skyline which tells the
Heart that home is but a breath away.

World's End
Charmayne Emmerson

It's cold here.
The wind takes my breath away;
Runs away with it laughing.
Gone. Lost.
Always windy.
The sea heaves and swells
Below the breakwater.
Grey. Dull.
Hidden secrets cower
In the murky depths.
I shiver.
With excitement, not fear.
I love it here.
Grim. Bleak.
Over the cliff and out to sea,
On and on to nowhere.
Nothing.
I feel small, insignificant.
Free.

A Squirrel's Year
Samantha Ellen Kelsall (8)

In the spring the golden squirrel dances round the beaming, bright
                                                    flowers.
She scurries round the tall, fresh trees.
Her coat, like velvet, catches light from the blazing sun and glows
                                                    with it.
Her eye flashes with amusement.
She frolics in the green fields showing all her glory.
As she lazes in the trees she gives birth to little, golden babies,
                                        happiness fills her heart.
That is the squirrel's spring.

In the summer the golden squirrel cherishes her beloved children.
The whole family is filled with splendour and charm.
They bound through the long, thin branches of the trees together.
Picking hard nuts and succulent berries, they dine as they go along.
They watch carefully for dreadful predators like the devious and
                                            cunning, sly fox.
With all the thoughtful mothers love she kisses her precious, darling
                                                    children.
That is the squirrel's summer.

In the autumn the golden squirrel's kind children disappear from
                                                    her.
In pain and feeling woeful she sheds tears of loneliness.
At the loss of her young ones she feels heavyhearted.
She clambers up the tree all alone.
Regretting letting her adored, new-born babies go, she sits in the cold
                                            on her own.
Dreaming of her little ones tears swell up in her eyes.
That is the squirrel's autumn.

In the winter the squirrel feels comfortable and calm again.
She dashes over the silver carpet of snow grabbing all the food she
                                                    can find.

Running back to her nest she stores all her delicious, appetising
                                        things in a secret hole.
In the chilly coldness she shivers and trembles as the frosty snow falls
                                        around her.
Suddenly her eyes begin to droop lower and lower.
She lies in her nest and falls asleep into hibernation as she waits for
                                        the beautiful spring.
That is the squirrel's winter.

          And that is the squirrel's year!

Ravello
J W J Collins

From orange groves, a scent that's sweet
The sun is warm, a gentle breeze
Some local wine, a lazy day
Down by the sea, relaxed, at ease.

Climb to the clouds, above the birds
And sample such tranquillity
This peace on earth, this heaven above
This perfect gem of Italy.

The soul is touched, to your surprise
The poet in you starts to rise
Like me, your words cannot explain
You gaze once more, then gaze again.

Hong Kong
Bruce Clark

The colonial ghosts
Take the governor's walk
Around the clouded peak,
Looking out towards the South China Seas
When the damp mist allows.

After their funicular slide
They take in the botanical gardens,
And the new tropic zoo
With which they are unfamiliar.

Then they take chattering tea
Beside Saint John's Cathedral,
With its cooling calm inside
And a tall, thin palm outside.

They do not take a sampan
Touring Aberdeen Harbour,
Nor the crowded, grinding tram
To nearby Kennedy Town.

The Lochen
Grace Tiffen

Soughing of wind through the trees by the lochen,
Redolent of sweet-smelling heather and whin.
Bracken like faerie-fronds nodding and dancing
In low-level counterpoint under the pines.
Scree on the brae tracing patterns in stone
As it skitters and scatters from under my feet,
Fleeing exposure in wind, rain and sunshine
To drown in the waters; conceding defeat.
Chameleon waters, reflecting the firmament,
Changing and shifting in shadow and light.
Scurrying, wind-rippled, busily bustling,
Or brilliantly placid as moon glow of night.
Air sweet and clear flights the call of the curlew.
Across the fine lochen it's singing to me
Of a land of courageous and bounteous beauty,
Where hearts never falter, and spirits soar free.

Majestic Mother
Lesley Curtis

Slumped against the corner
of an old pink sofa,
newspaper in hand.
Majestic mother
surveys life in her
assorted offspring.
Propped up on hard,
flowery cushions,
her life is a long round
of pans and powders,
soap suds and sobs.
She's a comforting oracle
of mother-knows-best.
Weekdays are workdays
and flowing washing
billows around her in
the flower pink garden.
She's a white witch
akin to mother earth,
enchanting spells and intricacies
of life only she knows.
Majestic mother sags around
the middle from the hard
joys of giving life.
She has sparrow footprints
dancing around her eyes.
She laughs deep and shrieks
with pleasure, loud whoops
bouncing around her home.
Majestic mother
is a colourful rag lady
tied to a well worn apron.
Wiping smudged hands,
she summons us to feast
spreading the well fed

feeling among all who
enter her ginger-bread home.
All may enter, all leave richer,
Majestic mother opens arms to all.

For Hilda

Enchantment (Clatteringshaw Loch)
Diana Tiernan

Moonstone sky over pewter lake,
cold thin wind through withered sedge,
and the wind raised waves
slap soundly on the shore

Tourmaline sky over ink-black lake,
icy wind lifts needle snow,
and the wind raised waves
chink bell-like on the shore

Pale azure sky over silver lake,
chilly wind through new spring grass,
and the wind raised waves
lap gently on the shore

Harebell sky over indigo lake,
soft warm breeze with heather scented,
and the breeze raised waves
curl cool around my feet

Changing sky over mirror lake,
magic air of turning seasons,
and the wind raised waves
come dancing to the shore

July New Zealand
Joy Roberts

Four tree-ferns grow by my window,
And a solitary blood-red camellia -
Out here, seasons are cock-eyed and beautiful.
Today I saw autumn leaves, cherry blossom,
Fuchsias and evergreens.
Wish one could trade, in retrospect,
Today's blue harbour view in winter
For every January day at home:
Five years now of bright winters
Building a settlement in my heart.

Innocence
Michael J Murray

There's a place I know,
A quiet land
Of white-capped silvery streams
And misty rain,
The kind that falls softly
Between the winds,
Shrouding the hills
And the secret places
Where only the Eagle lives,
A silent tree-bare ground
Sometimes bathed in a pale grey light
Revealing earth my grandfather knew
And haunted still by the plough and scythe,
And there,
On steel-hard winter nights
A candle burns,
For those who sleep
Forgotten
Beneath the pine-scented fields of my youth

Microcosm
Simon Wagener

Today on the bus I pass
the strange, distant building
that (from a bedroom window)
once formed the frontier

of my childhood, the margin
of my youthful world,
an unapproachable horizon
with all that its skyline cradled.

And though every new telescope
had drawn it closer and larger
it always kept its make-believe,
as if our worlds belonged on separate maps.

This time it's different -
a cold, simple, mocking fact
I shiver at its sudden nearness
the looming of its destination

knowing what has ended here today.

Negatives Of War
Ruth Bettany

Wandering through a war torn city
a million miles from home
documenting the abomination of desolation
to a passive nation.
The shells of houses stand butchered,
skeletal fragments point accusingly to a perfect sky
torn by a scrawled vapour trail
and below that ripped blanket-sky
are the shattered lives scattered
torn between fear and family.
   This could be a distant galaxy.
     The television watches back
     spitting facts
     meaningless to a materialistic mind
     capitalist corpse.
     The living room is hostile
     the chair uncomfortable
     even the furniture groans,
     take note,
     the floorboards creak
     and mourn.
These lives don't matter
to one suffering   care-fatigue
This is the bad news.
The Pure Unadulterated Bias.
Eternally affected, compelled to share their suffering
I don't eat   . . . again.
I bring home with me the negatives of war
and more than I can explain
images of the suffering anonymous and subhuman
I am tortured by uncaring civilisation
preoccupied with sex scandal.
The coathanger waifs pass me by
victims of refined culture.

I think of a bombed city
like a deserted scene of crime
nothing but a fingerprint,

at 5 stone 2
I pull the trigger.

Mother Of Protection
Jamie Shields (16)

Forever growing,
Forever sensing,
All curled up inside this warmth,
Listening to voices all distant but caring,
But unable to speak itself.

Protected, surrounded, covered but dumbfounded,
There's no safer nor special place to be,
Growing spectacularly,
Sensing emotions all from within this body.

Inside this tomb smothered by love,
The feelings of being secure and protected are so strong,
For this is the place where you couldn't feel safer,
Because you'll never again be this close to your Mum.

Dead-Lines
Anita Ewing

5.25 pm with deadlines is
Not the best time
4 her 2
Burst out from me, revelations all over Form AC162
And a startled passer by . . .
DELETE
I couldn't
CONTROL
Stay hidden hurting
MALFUNTION
Behaving all day, my body
Slipped from beneath her
BACK
I didn't scream. How I could kill she
REPEAT
And me jabbing the keys like eyes in watery sockets blood crying the
ceiling caves in
through wallowing nights and why she feels and feels that this is not
the ended end
back tomorrow bleary eyed
CHECK
I smile, at their smiling sorrow.
ERROR
Of dead flesh and memories,
Of trying to bury them
Amongst paper and
9-5.
Broken spirits slumped,
Painting
VOID
Stories on bleak canvasses
Missing
VDU
Feel space. Of trains and thoughts which get delayed
SPACE

Imagine Here   117

SYSTEM FAILURE
EDIT
Bitter coffee in dead-dirty cups.
Sleeping souls,
Wanting
U/2; ENTER.

END

Audlem
Joyce Marie Burgess

The cottage where my uncle lived was on a country lane,
With a twelfth century church across the road.
To a city child, then,
It was a magical place.
Another time. Another world.

Rooms in which the smell of tobacco
Mingled with the scent of flowers,
And a quarry tiled kitchen
Where my feet danced,
A fairy child bewitched.

I smelled the apples ripening in the loft,
Saw the cornfields bright with poppies;
Touched their red silkiness;
Picked the wild roses
Dreamed of princes.

I loved it through all the changing seasons,
Muffled against the chill winds
Or blackberrying in autumn
And walking by canals
Where dragonflies skimmed.

I went there last year to my childhood place.
Nothing has changed
As though time had stood still,
Holding my cherished memories
Safe for eternity.

Free Spirit
Lesley Kennedy

Listen to the sounds
Silver surfs
On oceans of waves
Breathless winds
With whispering birds
Flying high
With great freedom of delight
Shimmering shadows
Passing in sunlight
Reflecting to the soul
Looking on
Peace and Contentment
Of being alone.
A sight
A sound
A touch
Of what surrounds each and everyone
With this in your thoughts
Take a deep breath
Relax
We are all alone
But never lonely
Feel free with your spirit.

A Green Place
Reo Curle

Mona, Mother of Wales,
Proud and ancient Isle.
Resting place of unknown ancestors
On a stoney hill above Cemaes Bay.

A green place
A place of peace.
Somewhere to replenish and repair,
The distractions of everyday life.

Surrounded by
Wild seas and gentle seas,
Lapping on those magical shores,
Reflecting light and calming strife.

Disused copper mines
On the dark and brooding side,
Reminder of more prosperous times
When ships plied cargoes far and wide.

Haunting, mystical land,
Emitting strands of steel
Disguised as silken cord
To pull the traveller home.

Nostalgic Isle beyond compare
Where spirit does replenish and repair
A green place
A place of peace.

The Modern Garden
Sally J Russell

Already, the morning stirs,
the clear, crisp air, as yet
untainted by the day's emotions.
The evenness of brick, & tile,
the glint of sun on eaves & windows.

And, beyond all this, the hub of traffic,

never-ending.

The tragic garden lay
in darkened coolness;
never loved, discussed, or planned;
but plotted, as one plots a scheme -
'Something that will look after itself', they had said.

While they rushed to join the throb of traffic,

never-ending.

Celtic Pipes
Andrew McCabe

He played for us on Celtic shores
Tunes of a weekend dream with you
History watched you put your hand in mine
While the ghosts of scattered clans
Laughed with delight

We never will know his name
As he will never know his impact
One musician richer in his practice
Than an orchestra conducted
Among fairytales and lover's dreams

Familiars
Liza Hunter

When I think of friends,
moved, digressed, changed shape,
split in half, cell like.
Adhering to a person like a Siamese twin,
with my chameleon face I scrabble amongst you,
hurling out threads of friendship by the handful,
becoming attached.

It all takes so long and I have to be somewhere, someone else,
so I give back your threads wrapped up in a box,
and smile as I leave.

On the sleeve of my coat, hangs a thread like a hair,
left behind, I pick it off,
and store it away with my precious things,
sometimes I get it out, along with others,
and remember how attached I was to you.

Maybe by making one friend,
I become part of everyone that's ever been,
past, future, right now.

Everyone's familiar,
a man arranged in a chair,
the woman behind me in a queue,
a turn of head, a shape of nose.

I know you, I know you all,
you remind me of him, of her,
a friend I once had.

Writing to old friends,
how are you, weathers bad, what I mean is,
I met a man on the train, who knew you
a trace of yourself hung about him like cigarette smoke,

I wonder how you met,
anyway he had that thing, familiar,
it was like meeting you again.

Loch Ness, Scotland
Avril Ann Weryk

A vision of heaven, draped in a shroud
Of beautiful peaks and wispy clouds.
A haven of peace with a thoughtful grace
That wears the smile of a heavenly face.

What comfort you give with a whispered sigh
A feast of beauty to a watchful eye.
Your spirit of love flows true and strong.
To fill my soul with eternal song.

You're the core of my heart that inspires my all
To walk on the earth with ethereal soul
I can talk to you freely and tell you my schemes
The love of my life, the weaver of dreams.

When The Rivers Opened
Amanda Jane Martin

I walked alone abandoned in thought
lost in the past somewhere.
Then the tainted skies separated
until the vault of heaven opened.
A face of shimmering light appeared
as his breath moved me.
From the hands in which reached out
came forth the rivers of blood.
I began to move slowly, very slowly
as he searched inside my heart.
And in each room of my weary bones
he brought a lightness from darkness.
Of every single fibre of all my pain
he thus discarded into pools
of filled pleasure.
In the flesh of my heartbeat, and soul
he conquered all my flaws.
Thus I had become moulded into his
love, that had long since craved.
In the palm of his invited hand
I touched the depth of his wounds.
I stepped into his adoring eyes as I
felt his eternity feed upon me.
He turned the rivers over from red
and stirred them into a paradise.
Together we moved deeper and deeper,
inside the waves of bathed myrrh.
The colours of heaven danced into the
coming of a sunrise reborn.
And so I had been brought unto him in
another world,
of total love, total innocence,
and how we hypnotised . . .

Val D'Azure
Frank Beck

Briefly, we languished in the sun
Watched the days vanish as the week uncoiled
The silent mountains smiled
Provence welcomed and warmed us
We drank the wine, toasting tomorrow
Drowning the sorrow of departure
Saying farewell to Val D'Azure!

(Room 44)
Margaret Harvie

The concrete floor, grey, cold, unyielding, jack-boot loud;
The walls of crumbling brick, enhanced by 'Anglo-Saxon Blue'
Graffiti, superscribed on 'Institutional Cream';
Steel window frames, by vandals twisted into non-alignment,
Clutching plastic, plywood, polythene against the cold.
This is the so-called olive grove of Academe?

Asbestos-riddled Horsa Hut (post-war, pro-tem.!),
A den of dark decay, despair and disaffection,
(Speaks volumes to young minds of value and esteem
Giv'n to the Classics by this Mammon-driven world),
With leg-loose chairs, ripped roller-board, boor-battered books.
This is the so-called olive grove of Academe?

The ghosts of sages past, recorders of ancient life,
Philosophers, playwrights, scribes of wisdom, wit and woe
Let out in disbelief a suffering, silent scream.
The glory that was Greece, the grandeur that was Rome
Now huddle here; two empires in a Horsa Hut.
This is the so-called olive grove of Academe?

A dish of polished stones, the lapidary's art,
Shoots fulgent shafts to pierce th' environmental gloom;
And bold, defiant hyacinths release a stream
Of spirit- lifting scents into this barren place,
Where bust of Homer, sightless seer (now noseless), nods
In this, our so-called olive grove of Academe.

But there were times within that festering, scabrous cell
When spirits of the ancients breathed into our souls,
Their voices softly urging - 'Think! Reflect! and Dream!'
And, lifted on these timeless wings to higher planes,
We shook off the shackles and in breathless chorus joined -
'This *is* the hallowed olive grove of Academe'.

To A Lost Love
Catherine Rees

You walked so proud with swirling kilt
Glengarry cocked and dirk deep dagger thrust.
Brave smiling Seaforth, born to join the holocaust
Of war, with bayonet forced up to the hilt.
The pipes they urged you on with warring lilt
Your heart said no, but politicians - said you must.
The whole battalion now lie in the dust,
And we live on remembering how you blood was spilt.

The pipes they cried in anguish deep
As brave men to their deaths were sent.
You lie in Cyprus grove to shade you from the heat
With comrades to whose aid you went.
Mount Etna far above an angry watch does keep
Her belching lava's cry 'To late to repent'.

Ecstatic Living
Jamie Edgecombe

An eighteen year old, walks briskly about his business.
The scene: Times Square;
December; a high pressure system passes over head, but passive snow
still lingers.
Amid the morning bustle, a lone poet performs his work. The man
stops to listen:

Poet: 'Buildings the tower;
        trees watch the streets;
        humming humanity
        watches the trees.
        The birds escape; watch them all.
        And don't give a -

Passer-by: (Ah, I wish I were a bird;)

Poet: '-unshackled in towering trees,
        under corner offices,
        sixteen miles up;
        who watch humming humanity
        and look down upon the streets.
        They don't give a -

Passer-by: (Or do I wish that I was up there?)

Poet: '-While faceless is humanity.
        As the birds watch them pass
        with as much enthusiasm
        as they have for themselves.
        They are towered over.
        The snow merely dies -

Passer-by: (-Actually I don't care,
            I'd still rather be a bird.)

He strolls on, avoiding the city's shadows.
Reflecting on how the poet is life, and himself? Well, he's just him . . .
humming humanity towering.

Grandfather's Roses
Benjamin Tyree

Red roses in my grandfather's yard,
Gently raised by his rough hands -
Red as the blood of the man
And the fifteen generations that
Stretched before
Like a chain of consequence.
Now the roses climb the white-washed fence.
Neither Barbara Allen nor her Sweet William
Can avenge their wrong on each other,
Nor repent, nor repair
The damage of it
Though thorn and rose forever attach one another.

My grandfather loved his roses.
He had almost as many roses
As grandchildren young.
Summer after summer,
The grandchildren come:
The roses always come
With the sun.

A Sacred Place
Michelle L Dexter-Smith

A speedwell blue sky filled with willo'-the wisp clouds,
Carried along on a snail-paced breeze,
Drifting with lethargy past the swaying tree-tops,
With only enough strength to flutter their leaves.
A thrush proudly sings from a wizened old oak tree,
Easing weary travellers into blissful slumber,
Whilst doves softly coo from apple blossom branches,
Showering the earth with confetti pastels.

And so my eyes wander from glorious heights,
To a tranquil scene of emerald green,
Laced with gorse carpets and buttercup jewels,
Where dewdrops hang, like polished quartz crystals,
From a talisman modelled on the golden orb.

A trickling stream faintly echoes in the distance,
Gently lapping over time-worn pebbles,
Smooth to the touch, cooling to the skin,
Acting as a causeway through watercress forests.
And as I draw near, I see small stream-lined rainbows,
Gracefully gliding through clear crystal waters,
To protective shadows of gallant bulrushes,
Who stand like soldiers in leafy uniform.

Since childhood days this place has remained sacred,
An eternal monument of natural beauty,
Where I come to sit, to think, to learn,
Of all that life should be.

Distant Lands
Sue Thakor

Flying over dusty land
Hovering between mountain peaks
Then soaring into space, journeying onwards
Through fields of gold, poppy bright
Until they found land's end

Triumphantly they returned
Too their watery lands
And told a tale of adventure
Filled with sights and sounds
Strange to hear

Carrying sacklin cloth
They showed their treasures
Fruits from the south
And spices from the east

Soon as fruit and spices disappeared
All that was left was the story
Of distant lands
Handed down
From mother to daughter
A tale retold as generations passed
Leaving history in the making

The City Of Bath
M R Jackson

Underneath a frosty scale, stone arched and tempted a Georgian form
Finding resonance with a past time among the sulphurous warmth
Upon seven hills did the foreigners come to rest
And made their presence felt, buried deep amongst pilgrims
Those whom had heard, the power of Aquae Sulis
To ease pain of enlightened devotees

And the Roman ideal risen again
Given the basis of a place to be proud
Gone forth and carved the city with views
Revealed the force and steam which lay below
Exposed, a people indulgent in play
An outpost clasped by a diverse empire

For visitors, a must to marvel at all it has
Admiration of the theme for which it represents
Differing times casting a parallel
Encompassing a measured future with former traits
For some, to belong is to be respected
And to be respected there, is to belong

Winter's Child
Mary Elizabeth Hunter-Blair

Hot breath escapes in billows
as I run run run through the wood,
the world is frozen in winter
nothing stirs, only me in the wood.

The heart of the forest lies waiting
for the thud of my feet running by
and the poor little stream no more running
stares glassily up to the sky

The trees so majestic in summer
have one by one turned into knaves
they huddle together bent down with the snow
obedient to cold they are slaves.

I am happy in winter I sing and I dance
with a feeling of joy, I am free
the cold is my friend as well as my foe
I can fight it not like the poor tree

Static they stand with the snow at their feet
they are prisoners pathetic and numb
when my hands are held by the fingers of frost
I can loose them, throw snowballs and run.

That's why in the winter I run through the field
down the valley and into the wood
to the trees all alone and forlorn standing there
they might share in my own happy mood!

Spring Wood
Tina MacNaughton

A single dewdrop trickles as tender as a tear
Upon a golden bough it falls;
So pristine and so clear.

Silken scented snowdrops spring forth in wooded dells,
Triumphant yellow daffodils nod
To ringing sapphire bells.

Enchanted fairy glitter, silver threads of gossamer glisten
Dewy droplets gleam like diamonds
On shimmering cobwebbed ferns and thistles.

In and out of emerald vales, weave silver ribboned streams,
The jewelled goddess of spring presents
A golden valley of our dreams.

Echoes
Victoria Forbes

I enter the silent building encapsulated in time.
Summer has cast its life away
And now it stands forgotten and alone.
I trespass in futile hopes
Eager to turn the winds of time.

The college where we once loved
Is now lonely for its past.
With echoes of laughter, ghost-like whispers
Real yet intangible, resounding in my head,
I grasp the moment and drink it in.

I lie on the silenced field beneath the stars
That gleaned the lustre from my dreams.
The deft fingers of time have stolen pleasures
Yet memories remain concealed
Encased immortal as the sky.

A sudden gust of wind loosens a lock of my hair
And softly caresses my cheek.
The teasing air carries your voice.
It whispers my name
And I know that you are there.

Shell Bay
Carolann Dempsey (11)

The waves lapping against my toes,
The wind gently teasing my hair,
Sand flying about,
Green hills rise to the left and right.

Children run in warm tracksuits,
Yells and screams around me,
I climb the big grey rocks,
And sit on the grass.

Out to sea the ships go by,
I can see everywhere,
Leven across the bay,
Golden sand below.

The last rays of sun,
Capture the glinting sand,
The peaceful sea,
As a perfect photograph in my mind.

Fire

Christopher McParland

Fire is a prowling lion,
stalking on the planes.
It pounces from the hearth,
reducing houses into flames.

It's Ferocious claws
and vicious jaws,
rip the house to pieces.
The lion isn't an ancient myth
like the Argonauts and Golden Fleeces.

And on the colder winter's eve
the lion, no more trouble he weaves.
In its place Happy Men dance,
they are seen if into the fire you glance.

There comes a time at the end of each day,
when the fire dies
in the same old way.
The coals have been turned
for the very last time,
at the Witching Hour, the old clock chimes.

The Happy Men leave,
the lion dies.
Into the air, the last smoke
flies.

The Power In The Stones
(An Tursachan)
Douglas Johnston

Megalithic standing stones
igneous eternal
proud as pines
created in prehistory
in cruciform
by peoples from
Sun-stroked Iberian climes
souls drawn
to this harsh Northern land
searching solace
seeking the power in the Stones

Your children of Callinish
farmers seafarers hunter gatherers
worshipped the Stones
drawing
Cosmic energy
then
translated by the Shamen
by Astronomer priests
transmuted into
a vital healing force
such is the power in the Stones

Autumn Haunts
Nicky Hartle

I follow the curve of the mountain
with my angry eye
stillness shouts
through impressionable water
tainted by unresting invaders

I drag my boat through
incensed ripples irritate
dusk's red shadows
and sulkily they rest

Mist wisps past my tired eye
a haze is before me
behind the shady path is clear
with warm scents from the earth
and a comforting breeze
but behind lay the traps
overgrown pathways
the tamed responses
of a grey featureless hillside
and behind lays the memory
from which I run
floundering
scrambling
slashing through busy trees
to find a way through
my autumn haunts

Summer By The Sea
M Williamson

The storm has gone; the morning light, though dim,
Reveals a quiet sea, still leaden grey.
The beach, tide-wetted to the rocky rim,
Lies pristine smooth, awaiting children's play.

The dawning spreads; slowly a tentative glow
Brightens the eastern sky behind the brae,
Seeks the responsive window-pane, to show
The shining promise of a sunny day.

Then, clarified from silt, the morning tide
Will catch the rising sun, reflect its sheen
In sparkling waters, that no longer hide
Their myriad shades of turquoise, blue, and green.

The beach becomes soft-dimpled by the tread
Of children's feetc the marks of delving hands;
And parents, with their garish beach towels spread,
Relax, and snooze upon the sunwarm sands.

Clear shallow water tempts the most timid child,
Test with a toe, dabble a foot, then splash!
While bolder brethren, stirred by bravado wild,
Join macho friends in a mad, sea-ward dash.

Pack up wet swimsuits, brush sand from sun-tanned legs,
With cautious care the tangled tresses comb,
Eat the last sandwich, pour out the Thermos dregs,
Round up the children: time for the journey home.

Now one last guest, down in the sea-wall's lea,
Paused in a stroll that ends the summer day,
Enjoys the warm tones of sunset on the sea,
The cooling breezes rising from the bay.

The sun drops low; reluctant, the visitor leaves.
Turquoise and orange gleams still light the west,
House-martins swoop and pipe around the eaves,
Before retreating to their clay-built nest.

As dusk descends, the sea, more sound than sight,
Continues its gentle splashing without cease,
In distant repetition through the night -
A lullaby, to bring our senses peace.

Crainges Copse
Harriet J Kent

Herbaceous splendour hidden in a time warp of leaves
Gentle breezes blow soft messages of relief through the boughs
Of hazel, ash and chestnut, sunshine spatters darkened spaces
The evidence of bluebell corpses litters the earth
Amongst an herby odour of plantlife
Summer boasts an extroverted entrance into the copse
Creating shadows of warm yellow and greens
The distant call of a skylark awakens lost souls
Lost to the world years ago
The brief crackle of a twig sends echoes abroad
A signal of stranger to the pheasant who calls
A secret well kept is one never discovered
I'll venture back soon when I can, you know that

Swimming Pool Date
William Greig

Who is that synchro-slimline, sphinx-like girl
with the dark hair, bobcut style,
who pierced the bubble of my lonely swim
with her melting looks, intelligence and voice resonant with joy?

And, as we stood shallow-end, idle-Monday chatting,
our bodies seemed to warm the water like
the element of an electric kettle
which thawed my frozen, frightened but fun-loving little boy.
He tentatively asked for her name and company
in the after-shower and hairdryer bar;
where exchanging the 'I didn't recognise you with your clothes on!'
sportsman's quip and our love of the theatre, my spirits sang.

And now, I, alone among the bible-black audience, wait expectantly
for sylph-like Suzannah to sing and dance, perhaps just for me?

Arriving
Laura Cruickshank

Hard edged symmetry,
Of people and places.
Sharp shapes.
I follow the wind;
Rapid thinking,
Eyes smile at me
And set me spinning . . .

. . . To be crushed on hard faces
Of rock.
To suffer this change?
Pave the sea with moonbeams,
And I won't cry too long . . .
All red-eyes.

Leave me with the stars
And a hill to climb.

Field Of Remembrance
Stan Salt

I remember a field
Only a fence and a dyke away,
Spreading its open acres
Behind an ancient church.

On warm summer evenings
Ripening barley rippled
In declining sunlight,
With harvest in the offing.

Autumn tractor and plough
Gouged out fresh furrows,
Turning up choice morsels
For many a fidgety gull.

The rugged field piled white
Under winter's blizzards,
Whilst the bordering dyke
Maintained an icy presence.

I remember a field
Where often used to slog
Around its memorable margins,
Rector's lady and little brown dog.

Florence
Eileen Turner

Old city of narrow streets and fountains;
Churches, cool and dark and lovely;
Windows masked by patterned bars of iron
Wrought with skill.

City for the eye's delight;
Of deep sand-gold,
Of blue sky with high white clouds
Sailing over;

Of gentle people whose heritage
Is grace and craft and skill,
Smiled through and through
With love, to beauty.

Portree Sunset
Norah Jarvis

The waters of the loch lie mirror calm,
pink, mauve and grey,
under gathering clouds
lit by the dying rays of sunset.
Wrapped in a delicate veil of mist
threaded with fading hues of day,
harsh pinnacles of black rock soften
for a transient, heart-clutching span;
weave into the soul an illusion
of gently beauty and enchantment,
a promise of calm,
of eternal stillness
that suffuses all one's being
with unutterable peace.
Poignant tranquillity reflects
from the serene panorama;
unlocks the bonds of fraught mind and spirit
for a brief respite,
brief as this sunset hour.

Soon, his seductive magic gone,
Cuillin will stand silhouetted -
a harsh black frieze
on a menacing wall of luteous cloud -
terrifying in his unassailable power.

Tennyson Down
Beverley Beck

Chalky white cliffs reach out
And beckon to the sea below.
Each lap at their skirt is a promise
That infinite time will follow.

Berriedale Beach
Eleanor Hamilton

The kittewakes cloud the sky,
Moving fast and with purpose,
Dipping and diving deep.
Then, urgency dissipated, their food need met,
They rise and glide, alighting gently on the water.

Each spring a new dance begins.
Splashing, preening and displaying,
For their lifetime mates,
To excite, to seed the next generation.
Their call clear, vigorous, cooing and caring.

From mating dance to faltering flight
The young ones grow, tenderly nurtured.
Year after year
This ritual of regeneration repeated
Before they return to their wet wandering.

Suddenly they have gone and it is quiet,
Leaving sad reminders on the rocky shore,
Starved, mantled with feathers.
Each year fewer return; single, some perch on dried dead nests
How long will they wait for the one who will not come?

And as man ruthlessly clears the ocean bed
His ugly waste spewed landward by the sea
Desolate lies the beach
Will no kittewakes cloud the sky, nor dance each spring,
While jagged cliffs glower silent round the bay?

East Neuk Bay
C Drummond

Come let me taste thee
Salt tears curdling into creamy foam
Bitter kelp and sunbursts on the tongue

Come let me touch thee
Rough grained cut through by shattered shell
Eddies of sandy silk clinging and enfolding

Come let me smell thee
Smoking breath of gathered driftwood
Fragrancing the pot-pouri of pines and heady thrift

Come let me hear thee
Whisper words of a deep entwining
Blow passion's conch and storm the tidal drum

Come let me see thee
Gentle contours, dappling shadowed furze
Outstretched fingers pulling threads of lapis blue

A sense of place, time stepped in haar.

Polzeath
Brian Moon

We lay with the stately ease of kings on the turf of time,
While a whole orchestra of exquisite bells mimed
Their seasonal symphony in white beyond our sin-drenched minds;
The ebbing surf swayed soothing rhythms
To waft the strains of life into ethereal oblivion;
The menacing mouth of the moody Atlantic merely murmured
As the foam-sparkling sands bubbled,
Pristinely free of the transient mark of man and beast.

It was a moment in time where time's pulse flickered,
For we lay on the shadows of those before us,
In a place that had borne witness to laughter and to tears,
Where hopes had been lifted on the highest waves,
And tragedies buried in the deepest troughs;
Man had made his mark in this place,
But his influence was as fleeting as the
Sentinel sandcastle, standing before the relentless tide.

We left today with the warm imprint
Of a priceless jewel in our hearts,
But already, the crushed turf is rising -
And we are forgotten.

The Reunion
Beryl Birch

I am with the old crowd.
Basking in the glow of friendships
Cast in gold many years ago.
Forged with young energy.
Worked in patterns
From student days of
Fashion, music, romance.
Life loving, living for now.
Present pleasure, future fun.
Jewels of youth
Set in precious pieces.
Surviving the years.
A necklace,
Linking then to now.
Stretching across my life.
Girdling, entwining,
Twisting around me.
Strong, sparkling,
Loaded with diamonds of
Comfort, solace, support.
Lasting forever.

Sea Spray
Jeffery Wheatley

Raven and lichen-blackened rock
the slatey colours of the dark,

sea spray, blackthorn, campion
the white of winter come and gone,

primrose, gorse and celandine
the gold of summer come to spring,

bluebell, sky and blue-grey sea
the endless shades of things to be.

Watching And Waiting
Anders Larchess

Is it so long since
I trod the yielding sand,
surveying the towering cliffs,
the sweep of shoreline retreating
in twice-daily surrender
to the advancing tide,

saw stranded seaweed, shells
empty of life, sea cleansed
above the tideline
with sun-bleached driftwood,
flotsam of long seafaring,
randomly deposited?

I watched the dipping sun
make its daily exit
behind the curved horizon
of the endless ocean
and waited in the after-glow
for the night's star-studded show.

Again, I watch the sun
ham its rehearsed reprise
and, dimly in the twilight,
see garbage of a brasher age -
plastic bottles, condoms, cans,
black tidemark of an oilslick;

the scene transformed, polluted
by our impatient race
for greater creature comforts
and I wait, in awe, to see
if the stars remain unchanged,
or have they been re-arranged.

Vestigium
Ellis Griffin

I am the horse of the one-horse town,
I am an elm of Nine Elms,
An abolished king without a crown,
Who would care to enter my realms?

I am an oak of Sevenoaks standing,
Of Three Bridges I am the one
Minuetting, sarabanding,
Spanning time til it's finally done.

I am one of the Four Marks,
The other three are no more.
They wearied of my childish larks
And left me here to keep the score.

My Seven Sisters had always been
My bulwark against the tides
Washed recklessly across the screen
Of life's disjointed sides.

Displaced now, dislocated
From all my kith and kin,
I haunt the scenes they abdicated,
A single footprint leading in.

Halfway Round The Headland
Deborah Thorpe

In the Velvet Blackness of the Still Night
Under a Sky Carpet of Silver Stars
We arrived in metal at the Derelict Sight
And sat amongst the rubble
In a Symphony of Silence

Halfway round the Headland
Twisted Black Cables looked up
Through Broken Bricks.
Sand had heaped itself into Grainy Pyramids.
Looking
We saw only Beauty there

In this Cracked and Barren Homeland.
You reached across the Desert and told me
How many days had passed since our last visit
To each other
In this Kingdom of Chaos where You were King
And I your humble subject.

We made all kinds of Weather there
In your Kingdom where nothing could grow
But life could begin
And we sang until the Sun got up
When, blushing under its steady gaze,
Finally
You retreated.

St Mary's Island
Kevin James Moloney

Frenzied sea stampedes rocky walls,
Willing destruction to white washed stone fortress,
Lighthouse retains, defiantly through frowning sky.
Only sea gulls shrill and scream dementedly,
Spiralling the Island through salty spray filled air.

At this disorderly scene of nature,
Its wildness impossible to capture,
A photographer, mesmerised, looks on,
Familiar with the unspoken idea-such images,
Do not sell, within the tourist guides.

Avebury By Night
Jane Whittle

Stone faces grow flesh in the dark
at a private meeting of megaliths.

Accepting an old invitation
I approach with the moon at my back,

shake hands by placing a fist
in a cold, rain-hollowed pocket,

surprised by the sudden warmth
of a stout stone bear-hug.

From the Avenue into the Circle
I join the assembled listeners

and notice their inclinations
as carlight sets them in motion,

reversing their massive shadows
to race the clock backwards.

I catch the whole congregation
unaware of intrusion,

meet the assembly, and listen . . .
the stranger's footsteps are silent.

Retreat
John Crawford

Knit coherence in thought, if you like
Or let them wander, clouds could never
So aimless be.
For in the bower, so secret be,
Charms can be wrought, for everyday ordinary

     Whenever.

Embrace a moment, a capsule

     Whichever.

The Venus star, branded white-hot, eye-level.
The roosting flock, magnetic skeins dragged
Across rutted skies.
Craven light; timid veils; the iron taste of
Morning sharp - or leaden night.

It is all of one.

Appeasement now; solace then.

     Whenever
         Whichever
             Always
Sanctuary.

Reflections
Christina Hughes

It is like
Discovering your secret hiding place as a child
Watching embers glow on a moonlit beach fire
The excitement of your first kiss

In a whirl of old memories and warmest emotions
This love becomes all
And forgives all
gone before it

A spell is cast
As if pure magic
The champagne kiss of his hand in mine

I have been poured the drink of love
And in this glass holds the sweetest taste of happiness
I have ever known

Norfolk
Alex Polaine

Black fen of the winter,
Powerful earth untried
'Til spring unfolds its warmth
So deep, so far, so wide.

Land of wide horizons,
Distant farms and trees,
Golden fields of summer
Awaiting their release.

Broads of mills and wherries,
Reflections in the sun,
Reeds for man and creature -
Shelter hardly won.

Skies of patterned colour,
Air so rich, so free
At dusk's earthly meeting
Of sun and sand and sea.

Filey
M Aitchison

Sunshine across the balmy bay,
Majestic cliffs that stand to attention
And protect this ethereal time warp.
As I tread the cobbles past the fishing boats
Down to the golden sands,
Sands that time forgot.
Am I seven or seventy?
I seem to forget
For this is a memory
For this is today.
For the sand is eternal
And the tide of time held back.
And we are but travellers
In a micro second of time.

That Afternoon In The Garden
Wendy Ruthroff

The earth was loamy,
The nettles rooted long,
The dandelions in tutus
As I dug unearthing worm,
Centipedes and the blade
Of a disused plough.
I hastened to plant the seed
Before the day ended.
Was the earth warm enough?
Had we still frost to fear?
Mixed with sand, I
Scattered the seed,
Trusting that the sun
Would shine, the rain
Would not wash them away
That they would flower
And fruit in time.

Elegy For Venezia
David Green

Carnival eyeshades lace the windows here
In this miraculous water-threaded place;
A woman's art attempts a courtly face,
Cosmetic stroke of arch and step and pier.

With Gothic grey and gold and Roman white
The liquid walls swirl into fragments, while the light
Abetting all this work of guile
Dissolves the doubled steps
Along this mile of curious waterway.

This city might be an old courtesan, the one
Whose smile can still weave magic over man
Transforming us, not circe-like to swine,
But docile, wandering connoisseurs of wall
Of line and texture, domes, tall campaniles,
Flights of roofs and mirrored bridges all ablaze -
Till we become a 'gaze' of tourists in processional ways,
Aisles, sinister with gloom which hold their line
To the piazza-room and church clock's reassuring chime!

From Moise and Saint Job the chimes still fall
On the lagoon where huge cruise liners call
And powerboats tease, and tenders land fresh tribute on the quays.
The gondola-borne travellers now give place to those
In train or 'bus, and in they race past smoking furnace towers
Which set more grime and smut on the old lady's face:
So, slowly now with tears she sinks and her lace hemline
Might subside upon our sullied century's tide.

But still she works enchantment with decay
And day must see some able sons and daughters
To rule this fine conspiracy of waters,
And hold the piazetta floor between Saints Mark and Theodore!

An old Doge, meantime, peers through ancient stones,
Regrets, appalled, that flesh should quit these bones;
His plots and schemes what were they?, sighs and moans
Were they of no avail?; perhaps he sees
Processions in the corso tailing through
To ever new regattas lined with crowded balconies!
Above him still the pigeons fly, on the Ca Grande
Glows Apollo's sky; while this old man is listening
For a cannon sounding from the further shore.

Utopia
Stephanie Riley

A mountain high
A natural spring
A glimpse of snow
Peaked.

A swirling bird
high above
the shining sun
brightly.

A tranquil peace
and tiny flowers
a weightless cloud
drifting.

A feeling of calmness
of being at one
such wonderful sleep
I'm dreaming.

View From The Wood
D L Jennings

May-time yet clouds drift grey o'er the valley,
undecided where to shed their sparkling drops
upon the thirsty earth below. Above the clouds
a shaft of sun-light - but why no rain-bow?
Each droplet a prism flecked by sun-beams
a tiny prism - pure colours to arc across the sky.
I paused, from my vantage across the woods -
a floor-show, spectacular in its splendour -
was this a rainbow fallen from the sky?
Thus to lie broken in a riot of colour?
Blue, yellow, red and white flaunting
spring blossoms at their best -
still perplexed, the rainbow in its fall
true colours shed - the spectrum changed,
its complement accepted, red, orange, yellow,
green and blue with indigo and violet,
Richard of York indeed a colourful figure!
No longer the gracious arc across a stormy
sky-instead a gentle carpet of subtle
colours - spring flowers in fine array-
entry into Fairy-land-profusion of blue-bells,
arch-angels of yellow-random sprinkling of
red campions-stark against a back-drop
of virgin white starred ransomes-
wild garlic spread across the valley.

I Am My Special Place
M R J Ethridge

I am my special place –
For here, inside reside all memories;
Joyful, sorrowful, beautiful, spiritual.

Here dwell my joyful childhood days,
And nights atop the mountain peaks
Beneath the velvet ebony skies.

Here I cradle my new-born babe,
Awash with overwhelming love;
Reaching out now to a new generation.

Here my dear mother once again lives
Surrounding us all with her love;
Her memory bringing sweet consolation.

Here the sun's splendour kisses the sky
While ice flowers blossom on chilled window panes
And sweet scented meadows bring heavenly peace.

Though material things may crumble away
And aesthetic delights swiftly pass
It is here, inside me, lives the Reality of every special place.

San Francisco Twilight
Sanjay Nambiar

Twilight set upon my window,
beckoning repose through the memories of feeling
that lay latent underneath the romance and poignancy.
Twilight urged me to stay still,
to stop running from insecurity to strength,
back again, and to experience the windswept picture,
framed by the glittering loneliness of a city of dreams.
Twilight made me feel love again,
pulling me through my window into memory
and out to hope.

Esthwaite In Winter
J A Wearing

And should I see a casement glassed
  Embossed in frost no patterns planned
Yet not recall in wintering dreams
  The waking thoughts of childhood passed
Twixt hills that loomed in blinding white
  That rode astride the day in joy
Bearing the print of unshod feet,
  To peak the ridge pursuing light

Its crusade down icy valley plys
  Where shores in frozen awe abound
Becalmed in rigor's beauty set,
  Dead, but waiting, it tacit lies.
Beneath the pines that bind its edge
  Knights and warriors bend to shield
And dull the thirst of winter's pique,
  Proud and pursed their honour's pledge.

No rattle here, beyond lofted hawk
  Whose chilling swoop disturbs the air
Whilst cause provokes a plaintive cry
  To purge the scene, its silence broke.
And stirring now with brief, aware
  High reached beeches shake and shed
Their powdered egos in swirling storm
  In dignity, bled, their branches bare.

But as each lie precedes the dawn
  The dying spirit cedes its hold
Another maxim its curtain raised
  Treads the stage, with concept drawn.
Tho' dread the despot winter's reign
  Tho' harsh the tax, its levy base
Still fails to vie, refute or own,
  The thrust of spring, its challenge vain

Remembering Gordano
Jeanne Hoare-Matthews

Beneath the sloping woodland glade
sweet primroses grow in the shade,
so peaceful in their moorland home
the moorhen, snipe and pheasant roam.

Where misty moors and meadows meet
and waving summer corm lies deep,
where poppies dot the field like blood
and the farmyards always muck and mud.

When mellow fruitful days draw near
and autumn air is crisp and clear
the ruminating cows are fed
to prepare for winter days ahead.

Where eerie shapes from drifting snow
hide the hedgerow plants below,
the fierce frost freezes the horses breath
and the brown iron soil dies a cold slow death.
That is Gordano.

Standing By The Ocean
Susan Pearman

Listen to the voice

that changes every day

Watch the moving water

that never stays the same

Smell the salty air

the proof of where you are

And think of all the people

who will never get this far

Moonlight Negative
Ignas Bednarczyk

Incident for cameras hooded slattern gaze
myriad dimensions engrave
another net of times maze
to dig for ore to make a cave
spaces with ghosts
past and future continuities replete
beneath the glimmers pearl host
blazing bowed arches entreat
from thunders enfolding fire
where no mortal left the post
the soul impaled upon the spire
whilst the whip of oppresion is engrossed
pools of eyes bright as stars
bracken bellied clouds
bent bright bars
framed by oddly shaped silver shrouds
repeated as this with drumming start
rent the tiny hooks of jagged branches
when time changes and worlds part
Wonderlands giddy chessboard marches
cross hatched the beard
shaded this art
the future sheared
upon the tablet of Noah's heart.

Walsingham
Andrew Duncan

As an apprentice I had not much pay
but holidays I took on cycle thanks to YHA.
The hilly regions of the South Downs toured
and then the flat country of Norfolk explored.

I'd heard of the vicar of Stiffkey - a lady's man
(eaten by a lion on seaside pier), and of Fakenham
where race horses were bred and trained
and I like them on the flat pace gained.

A wise friend, Hal, told me of a small town
where long ago Richeldis, a lady of renown,
in a vision of Our Lady was willed
Nazareth's house of Annunciation a copy to build.

Like a pilgrim of old I came to the shrine
of ancient Walsingham where until the time
Henry VIII despoiled it, the halt and lame
from afar to adore and for healing came.

By the shrine a well, water blessed
and sprinkled on the faithful confessed.
Stations of the cross in the garden,
I joined others seeking peace and pardon.

That was forty years ago. Last September
I came again - many changes but I remember
things of the past visit which were still the same -
providing hope for the halt and lame.

Gone the days and cares of youth
but still I stumble on the way to the Truth.
Long dead is Hal but his spirit is here
in Walsingham, I will come again - this year.

The Pond I Know
P E A Richardson

There is a little pond I know, a quiet mysterious place
  Where newts come rising seeking air, and sticklebacks play chase.
A waterboatman skims the surface with a silv'ry track,
  While in the depths the caddis drags his home upon his back.

A tiny teeming world apart down there among the weeds,
  'Neath grassy banks, soft curtained by a tracery of reeds,
And to one side a mudslip, fringed by dairymaids of pink,
  Where through the mists of evening the cows come down to drink.

A thousand vital dramas each unfold there every day,
  Forget the strife o'er death and life, for this is nature's way,
But when the hand of man, with greed, rains poison from the skies,
  When plant and pond life perishes it is God's work that dies.

I pray 'twil never happen, or ever come to pass
  Some refuse laden vehicle may trundle cross the grass,
And there discharge its noisome load within this wondrous place,
  And make the little pond I know, a dump, a tipping place.

Where all too soon plant life would wither, little creatures die,
  The pond I knew oil filmed and lifeless, staring at the sky,
The only movement rising gas, no sign of fish or weed,
  Living treasure lost forever, victim of man's greed.

We poison all the airways, and pollute the living seas,
  We clear the land of brush and scrub and cut down mighty trees.
When will mankind realise for all his noise and fuss,
  We need this world in which we live - *The World Does Not Need*
                                                              Us!

A World Without A Window
Stephen Murray

Through the banister
And under the stairs,
Is a place of
Worn out boots
And old coats.

Through the banister
And under the stairs
Is a child's place
Of hide and seek,
A place
Of treasure troves
And dark scary monsters.

Through the banister
And under the stairs
Hide curled cornered photos
Piled high
Amongst records
Of vinyl
From yesteryear.

Through the banister
And under the stairs
Is a place
Of safety,
Of wonder
And of magic.

Through the banister
And under the stairs
Is the place
I'll be
When all else
Fails.

Never The Same
Anne Chisholm

There will never be another place the same.

All I need to do
Is close my eyes
And imagine the smell
Which creates it.

A small cottage,
And as I open the door,
The smell meets me.

A large kitchen,
And as I enter it,
The smell is stronger.

An open fire,
A black range and hob,
And, keeping warm on top of it,
A large blackberry and apple pie,
Cooked, sprinkled with sugar,
And smelling wonderful!

A rocking chair,
A smiling grandmother,
Resting, having made the pie
Because she knew that I was coming.

There will never be another place the same.

Thankfulness
Margaret Sawkins

It's strange, when once the mind is tuned
To notice all the little things,
How life seems full of treasure trove,
The darkest day is full of love
And thankfulness.

And so I've quite made up my mind,
I'm going to have a thankful day,
No grumbles, moans and heavy sighs,
No groans of protest, flashing eyes,
Just thankfulness.

I'll start as soon as I awake
To airy room and well sprung bed,
To fresh clean sheets of pleasant hue,
To warmth and comfort, green-treed view,
And thankfulness.

I'll savour that first sleepy stretch
Of healthy limbs and muscles firm,
Not take for granted eyes that see,
But gaze and gaze on blossomed tree,
With thankfulness.

To bathroom then with jaunty step,
With supple hands turn shining taps.
How good to start the day with hope,
And water hot, and scented soap,
And thankfulness.

Then spotless kitchen, window wide,
Birds on sill with feathers preened,
Bright beady eyes, awaiting crust,
Not knowing that I take their trust
With thankfulness.

To breakfast then thoughts soon will turn,
In loving, cherished company.
Across the cups of fresh brewed tea
Eyes will meet and he will see
My thankfulness.

My list of blessings grows apace,
Large and small they'll surely spread,
They'll give me strength and pave my way
To face this swirling, changing day,
With thankfulness.

The Dark Island
Sheila Broome

The dancers swing and swirl
To soaring Scottish strains
As pipers brisk and bright
In kilted tartan hues
Inspire the pas-de-bas
Of energetic toes,
The lively lift of legs
That keep the Celtic call.

Saluting shining swords
Upon the pavement placed
In busy Westgate Street.
Each step as light as lace,
Neat feet in shoes of black
And sporrans flying high
Fair melodies embrace
That please the passers-by,

And then the great bell tolls
From Gloucester's finest tower.
Now, as the pipers play
A haunting highland air
That hails the darkest isle
I listen, quite enthralled
And magic for a while
Pervades the city scene.

Whiteley Woods
Cynthia Stewart

As seasons come and seasons go
And time drifts by in endless flow,
The trees in Whiteley Woods stand tall,
Circling the village like some wall
Which keeps the noisy world at bay
And guards the stillness, night and day.

Yet life's astir beneath those trees,
Which flirt and whisper with each breeze,
As fox stalks rabbit, squirrels leap,
And twitch-nosed deer, with nervous peep
Of destiny's elected prey,
Emerges from his hideaway.

When nature, weaving magic spells,
Carpets the ground with bright bluebells
And bids the earth to do her will
With crocus, snowdrop, daffodil.
When feathered flocks fly in, to sing,
'Come nest in Whiteley Woods; it's spring!'

Sweet summer and a wayward sun
Mature the work spring has begun;
While autumn turns the leaves to brown
And sends them whirling, tumbling down,
Leaving the branches bold and stark
To wait for winter, cold and dark.

While seasons change and time goes by
And we live out our lives and die,
In Whiteley Woods, the trees still stand
Like sentinels in full command,
Holding the noisy world at bay,
Guarding the village, night and day.

Launde Leaves
The Leicestershire Wold
Patricia Mary Gross

The Launde leaves, are on the turn,
from green to red and gold,
as autumn casts her misty shroud,
which lingers o'er the Wold.
Launde in its autumn splendour,
beckoned this pilgrim, here.
For home is where the heart is.
This place, that I hold dear.
The pastel doves, fly overhead,
their pale, rear feathers fanned.
It seems, that they've descended
from that heavenly, other land.
The shades of autumn, splashed around,
attract and mesmerise;
giving inspiration and delight -
a joy, one can't disguise.
When 'er the mists, descend and swirl,
they encircle and consume,
could this, be like the arms of Christ,
when we're called from the earthly gloom?
The Launde leaves, that softly fall,
prompt the final tears, of grief;
And now, I must move onward;
In the strength, of my belief.
Of all the seasons of the year,
that grace the blessed wold;
the best, is surely autumn:
when the leaves, are red and gold.

After Beeching
Martin Summers

Here, where the tasselled catkins swing
and brambles impudently spring
up from the ground, then earthwards bend,
take root again and once more send
out thorn-snagged shoots. Here, where the sun
blesses the ash-trees, used to run
the Valley Railway. Trees encroach
where once proud engine pulled smart coach;
with brass a-glint and paint a-gleam,
a plume of smoke, a wisp of steam,
the little loco trundled on
from Exeter to Dulverton.

So punctual, so convenient,
the busy little engine went,
carrying half a county's needs -
cattle cake, fertilisers, seeds,
boxes and bags and bales galore
and country people by the score.

Now there is little that remains
to trace the trackway of the trains.
Permanent way's decaying fence
testifies its impermanence.
But, masked from all save searching eyes
by weeds' wild carpeting, there lies
the ballast that upheld the shock
and weight of jolting rolling stock.

Countrywide were the railways raped
(has any local line escaped?)
and we've exchanged the iron road's small
landscape incursion for the sprawl
of livid scars on every hand
where concrete swallows farming land.

What valid reason could support
destruction of this wanton sort
(relying, lest we felt deprived,
on figures carefully contrived)?
What benefited from the cost
of losing all that has been lost?
Progress? Such progress as is seen
is lemming-like of Gardener.

The Orphaned Cottage
Anthony Stern

The pond looks different now
All cloaked in weed
With no room left for small boats
And home-made rafts
To sail to where the pirates are.

The cottage I remember
Looks empty now
With its boarded-up windows
And vandalised doors,
And I feel its sad and modern emptiness.

The trees are the same
And the broken-bricked wall
Where spiders and ants
And even sunbasking flies,
Could be briefly tricked into ownership.

And I can shut my eyes
And listen out
For childish cries of indignation
At being dragged home, too soon, for tea.

Then I was ten;
But now with life's
Incorrect way of adding-on the years
I am fifty and grey,
And do not feel comfortable enough to stay.

Yet as I walk away
From the orphaned cottage
Across the pond
To catch my adult-driven bus,
I look back and see, after all, what I came to see.

My favourite place
Is a pond by a ruined dwelling
And surrounded by trees
That do not quite mask
The battering engines of passing cars.

Yet, the orphaned cottage
Has far more in common
Than anything else,
For a boy without a mum and a dad
Who once lived inside it, along with his gran . . .

Glasgow Central Station
Helen Dalgleish

Victorian, imposing, familiar –
tall, soot-stained columns form a cobbled cloister
where square, black taxis drop and pick up passengers –
excited, impatient, purposeful.

High, cathedral, glass ceilings
let in the light,
subdued by the dust and grime
of a hundred years,
so sun and cloud make little impact
on those hurrying and waiting below.

Flakes of rusted paint precariously hang,
picking their moment to fall,
but are good naturedly brushed off
by targeted travellers.

Illustrated by blobs of flattened chewing gum
and coloured litter
dull, grey platforms routinely greet
the tired, shabby trains.

A retching escalator
spasmodically spews
streams of commuters
from the lower level.

Against the glinting background cloth
of white marble flooring
transitory silhouettes flow by,
alone or in groups,
and the warm bustle of humanity
hangs in the air.

Spirits jostle with the living
and ghosts linger.

The smell of steam is only a deep breath away.

Clutching a bucket and spade
a little girl runs gleefully
by her grandmother's side
to board the busy seaside train.

And a young women
pensively stands by the shell
waiting for the lover who never comes.

Sunset At Polruan And Fowey (Foy)- Cornwall 1992
Christine Cluley

The gulls swoop, screaming their goodbyes to evening sun whose
                                            farewell bow
Dips 'neath Ready Money's trees.
In gown of brilliant amber gold, she trails her hem into the bay
And floats her ribbons on the breeze.

Yet still the little orange ferry chugs its way like wind-up toy
Twixt the gently bobbing dinghies, harboured safe alongside Fowey
                                            (Foy),
Sail-less yachts await tomorrow and the promise of new day
Pilot boat still guides the passage of larger boats of china clay.

Carelessly tumbled cottages cling like limpets to the past,
Caught in the peace of stillness when God's fishing net was cast.
Breathless tourists step the heights to cliffs o'er Lantic Bay,
Where beauty and majestic views take their last breath away.

And gulls will call and fisherfolk will work the watery deep
While morning sun and evening shade shall Cornwall's secrets keep
But we will see in recesses kept hidden in our mind
The towns of Fowey and Polruan that we must leave behind.

The Tree
Emlyn Jones

In a clearing in the forest stood a solitary tree,
Its strong and powerful stature was what a tree should be,
Free from disease and healthy, each crisis it survived,
While some of those around it, fell foul of pest and died,
Despite the years its canopy showed little sign of age,
Its limbs had not been broken, when wind and storm rampaged,
This tree was blessed by heaven, its existence not denied,
Its pleasure was in living, and in living, satisfied,
Each day brought new horizons dawning visions unsurpassed,
But as with all creation, simple pleasure does not last,
It knew the curse of lightning, perhaps a woodmans saw,
No matter what but something, would make it bend and fa,
And then one day a sapling, growing nearby to the west,
Began to bloom and ripen, showing beauty at its best,
The tree looked down in wonder, as the sapling looked above,
The sapling flower lay open, its expression spoke of love,
The tree knew no resistance, as it rippled with desire,
What began as mutual interest, soon became a forest fire,
Out of control and helpless, the tree dropped pollen seed,
And on the breeze they floated, to the saplings craving need,
In a clearing in the forest stood a solitary tree,
It now has two companions, and the clearing now has three,
In a clearing in the forest stands a proud and happy tree,
For the sapling it was Susan, and the tree, you see, was me.

Return Flight From Jakarta
Richard Glevum

I've seen the land of thirteen thousand islands,
The emerald girdle of the eastern bride,
The giant steps striding from Tanjung Priok,
The hooded mountains where the old gods hide.

Cu-nim at thirty thousand feet, bright violet arcs
Crackling and dazzling through translucent shroud -
Split Krakatao, Palembang's muddy river,
Volcanoes smouldering through purple cloud.

I've known the vibrant city's morning thrill,
My heart beats quickly at the Kretek smell,
The call to prayer, the sirens' urgent shrill...

Bright lights of Singapore, the flaps unwind -
Oh, gentle smiles, the last touch of farewell:
I leave, as if I leave my heart behind.

My Scotia
John H D Robertson

Wandering the drought-stricken bushveld, content yet lonely too:
The African sun blazing down on the land; out of a void of
blue.
Then I saw the distant mirage, with its trees and a loch so cool,
And my thoughts and heart fled homewards; to Scotia and Ullapool.

Once again I saw the village, the harbour and the boats at rest,
With dusk settling o'er the water and the sunset pale in the west.
Once more I saw the lights aglow; on the masts of those fishing craft
And memories sped down the years with the force of a cross-bow
shaft.

In fancy I saw those trout aleap; in the rush of a highland stream;
So vivid, so real, so wonderful. O Scotia! How a Scot can dream.
Look there in the brown clear water: is that not a salmon at rest?
Is that not a stag on the hillside, symbol of the land I love best?

In my dreams I saw the mountains; so grim, forbidding and grey,
With the scudding hosts of rain-clouds; where only the eagles play.
The banks of mist now sweeping; all but those peaks from view:
O! rugged land, O! wild land, how love for Scotland holds true.

Love for the glens of my forbears, love for the simple and true,
Love for a land that bred courage and such wondrous poetry too.
Love for a land of great principles which also black treachery knew.
Love for Scotia, its peoples, its moorlands and its lochs so blue.

Now that I'm old and weary, with hair bleached white by the sun,
Now youth has been squandered and I've hung up saddle and
gun,
Let me hear the pibroch calling, hear it calling me home once again,
This time to rest forever, beneath North Star, heather and rain.

Guildford
Sally Browne

Apple trees, gardens and bridges and boats,
Willows and meadows and marshes and moats,
Thistledown, cobblestone, solid oak doors,
Bracken and heather, soft covered moors,
Rolling hills, churches, town hall and clocks,
Rivers and arches, Weir House and locks,
Roses and daffodils, dandelion heads,
Daisies, wild rabbits, and tame flower beds,
Shining wet slate stones, dark clouds and rain,
Pilgrims mud paths, dull narrow lanes,
Red sands, old abbey, fair grounds all bright,
Markets and brownies and grave yards at night,
Fog lights, snow flakes, folk art and parks,
Barges and woodlands, starlings and larks,
Robins and sparrows, a squirrel, a mouse,
Fields below attics, a wondrous dolls house,
The hundreds of bridges, the many old halls,
Alice in Wonderland, museum's four walls,
Snow on the mount, tree houses too,
Chicks stuck in pollution at the Yvonne Arnaud,
Laura Ashley bedrooms, coal holes and cellars,
Lunch with Great Granny, tea at the Kellars.

Land Ahoy
Laura Warburton

Blue, water, deep, death,
Ice, cold, winters, breath,
Swish, sway, feeling, ill,
First, aid, no, pill.

Sailor, handsome, cute, tie,
Stupid, thick, plane, fly.
Food, vomit, green, face,
Quick, brandy, strong, taste.

Ahoy, land, anchor, quick,
Too, late, up, sick.
Land, hot, relax, pool,
Gin, costume, keep, cool.

Enough, burnt, drunk, pack,
Now, here, go, back,
Body, sore, raw, pain,
Oh no! Boat again! ·

Rivington
Kathleen Hinks

Lancashire village in history steeped,
Your beautiful scenery in my heart I keep.
Tranquil lakes, so peaceful and calm.
Lend eerie stillness, a soothing balm.

Leafy woodlands with shady nooks.
Gurgling streams and babbling brooks.
Darting minnows and hovering dragon flies
A flash of blue as the kingfisher dives.

Carpets of bluebells fill my mind's eye
A memory of springtime which never will die.
Summertime days, carefree and bright,
Childhood picnics of pure delight.

Autumn glory of colourful hue.
How could my heart ever let go of you?
Tumbling leaves of gold and red,
Softly whisper, it's time for bed.

Winter hovers to clothe the country scene.
The bare landscape shivers, stark and lean.
But snowflakes dress her in a gown of white.
Creating a wonderland of shimmering light.

The seasons depict the passage of time,
Along life's journey, they fall in line.
From childhood to death, our memory recalls.
The times in our life we've loved most of all.

Your gentle call tugs at my heart
And beckons me home no more to part
From your whispering breeze and meadow sweet smell.
I loved you more than words could ever tell.

Circus
Kathy M Tupper

Nomadic, cramped, small spaces.
Sea of faces, expectation great and small.
Smells, grease paint, sawdust, horses
Running, costumes gleaming.

Laughter, shrieks of delight. Red noses,
Black eyebrows, orange, fuzzy hair. Sand,
Water, trumpets sounding. Excitement,
Music, noise.

Always moving, hurrying. No time to delay.
The show must go on. Balloons to display.
Crowd laugh, gasp and sigh. Shoes too
Large. Oops, watch out! Another
Bucket of water tips out . . .

Children's laughter fills the air. It
Heightens the expectancy. The crowd
Hoping to see, maybe, a touch of
Tragedy.! The high-flyers soar above
The crowd, faces uplifted, breath held.

Gasp of wonderment at it all. I
Walk across the circus ring, distant
Laughter in my ear.

Take off the make-up, grease and hair,
Powder, paint - look in the mirror.
What is reflected there? - Sadness
And a silent tear, for behind the

Mask now stripped away,
A man looks back into his face,
Reflected as it seems in time
And space. For he is as no
Others see him -

A lonely clown!

My Favourite Place
Jo Spencer

My inner world is my favourite place,
Where I can escape to, and find the space
To ponder on life, understand my fears;
The endless questions that, through passing years,
Have challenged, teased me, driven me to tears.
I speak to no-one, so nobody hears.
Yet I know they'd understand the reasons why,
In the recesses of my mind, I cry
For the answers to questions that have none,
And muse on concepts that defy reason.
I am besieged by emotions that tear
At the heart of my being. I despair!

And yet . . .

My inner world is a sacred place,
Where imagination is filled with grace
And beauty. There all ordinary things
Are transformed as if by magic. My heart sings!
There the heavens are a shimmering blue,
With startling shades of every hue;
The rich earth sizzles with tropical heat;
Ochre fields ripple with ripening wheat;
Rare flowers bloom in endless profusion,
Rich carpets of colourful confusion.
Undulating hills, majestic mountains;
Crystal clear streams, cascading fountains.

My inner world is beyond another's control.
Despite the paradoxes, it's where I feel whole.

Wells Next The Sea
John Guy

It's hard, as one gets older now, to go away.
The fire-side chair pulls cosy as the dusk comes in.
The simple and familiar fill a summer day,
So, I am often tempted as the thought drums in,
To stay at home and never go adventuring.
And yet we did!

Wells next the Sea. In Norfolk light
The mud-flats bear the angled shapes
Of boats waiting the tide.
On Samphired shores we marked the sunburn flight
With sea-bird hands. Took walks where one escapes
The penetrating tang of sea-food, fried.
And there we tasted salt upon our lips,
From un-accustomed packs of fish and chips!

Bells next the quay. This morning, mist,
Antique shops musty and the tea-shops crammed.
The sun conspires to hide
But we ignore the wind's erratic fist.
Down by the coast-guard hut, beyond the tide,
The masts still list.
And yet 'tis heaven here. A man has ease
Where little pennants wrestle with the breeze.

Spells ecstasy? perhaps I might
Permit myself extravagance of phrase
At in-expensive times.
For did we spend more hours than cash
Upon this beach
Where nature chimes
A peal of promise to return?
You bet we did!

Journey
Dorin Dent-Axelsson

I was early that day.
I stood on the platform waiting,
enjoying the fresh morning
filled with spring's special fragrance.

A carpet floated by
shimmering with bright colours,
but it was occupied and
the passengers waved a gracious goodbye.

In came the train and I stepped in
moving away from the free-styled youngster
whose head was already vibrating with loud
tsk, tsk, tsk, tsk . . .
to a far corner seat.

I had my book but didn't feel like reading
so I peered out into the half-misty landscape.
The train had its rhythm
soothing and hypnotic
bideldedee, biddideedah, bideldeedee,
bideldedeededah . . .

I drifted with the melody and my fantasy
roamed through enchanted realms.

When I came to my journey's end
I left the train
Smiling.

In The Beginning
Basil Christian Nielsen

In the beginning the Bible states,
Genesis, chapter one, no date.
But God created Heaven and Earth,
Gave light for day and darkness night.
Today we prophetly believe it saith,
That Christian words are full of fai-ith.

In the beginning South Pacific way,
The Morioris roamed around all day.
Until from Polynesia Maoris came,
In large canoes, weren't they game.
Ao-tea-roa, Land of the Long White Cloud,
Today, New Zealand, a country proud.

In 1642, a Dutchman came,
Abel Janszoon Tasman was his name.
He chartered coasts but did not land,
Australasia roughly planned.
Today Tasmania and Tasman Sea,
Named after him in honour be.

In 1769, Captain James Cook arrived,
An Englishman forever strived.
Tried to land for food and water,
The natives did not think he orta.
And so he named it Poverty Bay,
No refreshments got that day.

Cook sailed on, a desperate measure,
Certainly no time for pleasure.
At last arrives at a safe haven,
Maoris friendly, gave provision.
So Bay of Plenty it had to be,
Mount Cook and Straight in honour, see.

In 1840, at Waitangi,
Another beginning, bells did rangi,
When Maoris and Pakeha signed the Treaty,
Natives and Whites to live in peacie.
Now British Empire and Queen Victoria,
Gloria! Gloria! Gloria! Gloria!

In the beginning 'twas '23,
I was born at last to see,
Kiwis friendly, a happy home,
No need to further more to roam.

If I . .
Rob Cotterill

If I could tell you,
I would.
If I could show you,
I should.
Let me look into your eyes
and express myself.

Your beauty is without equal.
Your compassion is beyond
that of mortality.
If I am the darkness
surely you are the light.

What brings two people together is unknown.
What unites two souls in the
heaven of love is a mystery,
but if there is one truth
our journey will always be together.

The Daffodil Line
Elizabeth Brace

Through the countryside it ran
a long snake-like track of steel grey,
along it puffed the steam train
our metal roaring giant of yesterday.
At Ledbury Station, Mr Brookes,
Who was Station Master in those days,
watched the passengers embark
each upon their separate ways.
On leaving the Station - left over the bridge
down to the Halt in Bye Street.
Late comers running down the path
clinkers crunching under their feet.
Out of the Town, through fields by the River Leadon
And close by Upham House.
Then arriving at Greenway Halt
which was usually as quiet as a mouse.
Past Taskers' cottage at Anchor Bridge.
Down a daffodil lined straight
to Dymock Station with its beautifully kept gardens
Mrs Badham waiting, watch in hand, lest the train be late.
Staff. Jess Carter, Bill Rogers, Signalman Mr Pollard,
Station Master Mr Wilce to name but a few
and of course Engine Driver Jack
and all the various footplate crew.
Milk churns to be loaded
a crate of chickens brought for Stallards Place
hopefully they will boost the egg collection
and bring a smile to Mrs Hawkins' face.
On towards Fouroaks Halt
past the canal so dark and green,
in spring the railway banks were yellow
all the daffodils were a sight to be seen.
At last the train puffs into Newent Station
with the Station master standing patiently by
when all goods and passengers were safely off

only then did he give a cry.
'Any one here for Gloucester?'
Alas this country line did not last
not since Dr Beeching used his axe
and made our daffodil line a memory of the past.

Maracus Bay
Sati Sen

The pale blue sky
near Maracus Bay
the endless crystal water
flowing gently against the coasts
                    with laughter.
Tall coconut palms line up
on unspoilt wide sandy beaches
                    swaying gracefully.

Several turtles head up
   to look for nesting sites.
Wide boundless pale blue sky
   reflects on the rough Atlantic.
Hungry birds' beaks catching fish
   northern range behind still like statues.

Amazing colours of the birds
                    mysterious wetlands
their spectacular beauty
                    and tranquillity
remind me the truth
and reality of nature.

Love and happiness
   come over me,
a voice inside says
   this is Paradise.

My Special Place
Ruth Bibby

The bedroom, the sleeping chamber,
Is my favourite place,
For, out of its window, the plain,
Un-enhanced view is familiar from teenage years.
There used to be apple trees -
A tiny orchard - in the garden next door.
Now, they're all gone.
Just grass and one particular tree
Grow there still,
Before broad commerce,
With its appetite for cars,
Creates a parking place
For me to dote upon instead.

Autumn Roses
Elena Johnson

October now and still my roses
                    bloom
Whilst autumn in her sad beauty
Does creep toward the winter's gloom
And everything in nature pauses now
To savour fading memories of
          summer not long gone.
And watching waiting, whilst the
          blossoms take their gentle bow
Oh! how much longer can my roses stay
To hold the shades of winter days
                    At bay

The Place I Often Go
David Clarke (16)

The place I often go is as light as snow.
Visited at night where only I can go.
The things I see, feel and touch doesn't always make sense.
But my place is my place where only I can go.

I'm there again, I see a face, the face of a woman,
A face with the deepest of blue eyes as blue as after dusk,
A face with hair so blonde but so dark it's nearly brown.

I'm dreaming again, of what I do not know,
I'm riding, I'm riding a massive roan stallion with brown glossy hair,
I'm in black armour, the blackness of night is within,
I carry a sword in my hand, the sword is alight with a light blue

azure.

I'm dreaming again, of my fair lady,
She is standing alone in a white dress a whiteness of snow.
Her face is a flower that will not wilt,
Her face is a flower that makes a fair rose like a thorn.
Her skin is whiter then snow so much that to her complexion it's

cream.

I'm dreaming again, of my fair lady.
She is being approached by two men whom I do not know.
She is being beaten, having life taken out of her,
I swing my massive sword which is afire with anger.
It crunches as it hits the first.
It crunches through metal and bone, his head is a roll.
The other comes at me from behind, I'm knocked from my saddle.
I turn and look into hell,
I swing my sword, it sizzles in its blood, it sizzles in hell itself.

I'm dreaming again, though a thousand years have past,
I look at the world today,
I see trees as stumps of white dust,
Alone is all I feel,
The world has died,
I look down at my hand, I see bubbles in and under my skin,
My hand is on fire though there is no flame.

I'm dreaming again, though I have died,
I see white light all around.
I'm on a cloud though way above,
I see my fair lady, asleep, the one I left a thousand years before.

At The Cove
E Gray

The sun and rain,
the hills and the ocean
give way to the light
of the secret white mansion.
A river running down to the beach
slips over stones and whispers like children.
Blue skies are warm with soft, rainy shadows.
The freedom! The I am. The soul life
through windows of time at the cove.
Rocks covered brown with debris and seaweed,
a treasure chest open, glinting jewels and stones;
colours unfolding the rush of the tide to remove.
And speaking, speaking, a big wide sky.
Holiday moments soon pass me by,
but now in the thinking
thinking,
with my heart so open,
singing and singing
the song of the cove.

The Big Sea
Ani Mota

If I never do anything
Let me get this right.
I'd feel too much
To have to stay and
Wile away your days.

I wondered how it feels
Sitting there, and all the good times
Hurt so, so, much.
So, she'd shed a tear for the time
She's lost.

All you want to give -
And narrow boats in London,
The local shops,
And Mother Nature's children
Scent the heather and watched
By passing trains.

A Christmas kiss
I'll never forget.
And I swear I'll feel

My lips when you're gone.
But nothing will console me.
And now I know there is no God,
Not even yours (except for you).

You'll die with me and not before.

Do you pray for every day?
Thank your lucky stars?
As brief as it was
I can feel your loss.

Her children see
The purest form of life.
Their children will never forget.

So if only I could avenge
You of your attackers.
And if they were made to feel
Just half of your pain

They'd fall in on themselves
And fill the stale air
With what they'd learnt
And take it to their graves.
And burn, exquisite

Golden flames
To warm your heart.

Small Moments Of Time
Judy Balchin

We had found the most Enchanted place.
It was as if it had stood still in time forever.
We would go there as often as we could.
Just to sit and be alone and forget every day things.
Just for a small moment in time.
If time could stand still we would have stayed forever
In our Enchanted place.
And inhaled the sweet smell of bluebells and moss and
The fresh green pine trees forever.
But just like the tide of the sea time cannot stand still.
We must move on.
Back to our everyday lives.
But still we know that we have our Enchanted place to go.
When life gets a little tough.
If just for a moment of life's time.